MONEY
MANAGEMENT

*Get Out of Debt, Make a Budget, Save Money
and Learn the Steps to Building Real Wealth*

MARK MILLER

©**Copyright 2015 Great Reads Publishing, LLC - All rights reserved.**

This document is geared towards providing exact and reliable information in regards to the topic and issue covered. The publication is sold with the idea that the publisher is not required to render accounting, officially permitted, or otherwise, qualified services. If advice is necessary, legal or professional, a practiced individual in the profession should be ordered.

From a Declaration of Principles which was accepted and approved equally by a Committee of the American Bar Association and a Committee of Publishers and Associations.

In no way is it legal to reproduce, duplicate, or transmit any part of this document in either electronic means or in printed format. Recording of this publication is strictly prohibited and any storage of this document is not allowed unless with written permission from the publisher. All rights reserved.

The information provided herein is stated to be truthful and consistent, in that any liability, in terms of inattention or otherwise, by any usage or abuse of any policies, processes, or directions contained within is the solitary and utter responsibility of the recipient reader. Under no circumstances will any legal responsibility or blame be held against the publisher for any reparation, damages, or monetary loss due to the information herein, either directly or indirectly.

The information herein is offered for informational purposes solely, and is universal as so. The presentation of the information is without contract or any type of guarantee assurance.

The trademarks that are used are without any consent, and the publication of the trademark is without permission or backing by the trademark owner. All trademarks and brands within this book are for clarifying purposes only and are the owned by the owners themselves, not affiliated with this document.

WAIT! – DO YOU LIKE FREE BOOKS?

My **FREE Gift** to You!! As a way to say **Thank You** for downloading my book, I'd like to offer you more **FREE BOOKS!** Each time we release a NEW book, we offer it first to a small number of people as a test - drive. Because of your commitment here in downloading my book, I'd love for you to be a part of this group. You can join easily here → http://yourcashmanagement.com/

Table of Contents

My story 8

Money Management Benefits 11

The Importance of Saving and Budgeting 15

It's hard time Managing Money 18

Types of budgets 20

Budgets for individual 22

Step Budget Making Process 24

Top Budgeting Apps 28

Steps to follow when making a budget
      for an irregular income earner 34

Controlling expenses and how to spend less 36

Ways to make extra money 40

Budgeting and Debt Management 42

Care giving and Money Management 45

Teens and Money Management 48

Money Management For Couples 51

Credit Counseling and Debt Management Programs................54

How Debt Management Programs Work.................................55

Things to ask before Enrolling in a

    Debt Management Program: 56

How To Manage Your Finances Properly And Improve Your

    Lifestyle-Money Management 61

Money Management Tips to Avoid Bankruptcy 64

Budgeting and Cash Management 67

Why Money Management Is Vital To Futures Trading Success 70

Top Tips on How to Budget Your Money 74

An Essential Tool For Money Management-Budget Planner...77

Money Management For Financial Comfort............................80

Money Management By Creating A Budget 82

Building Strong Money Management Skills............................85

Learn Money Management Tips 88

Money Management Starts With Budgeting 90

Effective Money Management 93

Money Management Software 96

How to Create a Money Management Plan 99

Money Management Means a Budget 102

PPC Money Management and Blackjack 106

Personal Money Management Guide 110

Effective Money Management Tips for a Better Life 113

When Money Management Habits Need A Boost 117

Tips on Money Management During Economic Recession ... 120

Money Management Tips For Career Changers 125

Can Money Management Help You? 126

Approaches To Manage Your Money 127

Debt Reduction-Money Management 131

Money Management for Wealth Building 134

Eight Money Management Essentials 137

Budget and Credit Counseling 140

Options for Money Management Help 142

Money Management With No Excuses................................145

Money Management 149

Conclusion..153

My story

My dad was born in a poor family, his parents were farmers. He got a job as worker in a factory and years later he quit that job. For 6-7 years he was unemployed and during the depression period, his mother sold everything to save the family. After that depression, they became cautious about money and they realized if they don't have a plan, they would end up being poor. So when my parents got married, they had a clear purpose on mind to work hard and save more money. My dad sold sandwiches in a college along with his business partners in a van. They were poor but ambitious to make money. So this business gave him some money for other savings or investments. He bought a piano from the college, the university was selling the piano which was old and it was sold at a discount price. He was able to buy it and made it like new one. He sold it a profit which can buy four old pianos; it was great selling at profits during that time. He did everything legal, so no one can question him

It is good to look for opportunities even in the tough times and increase your income. Years later I happened to follow their rules of saving, investing money. They actually inherited the ideas to me. There ideas were simple and strong to make anyone rich. They calculated the risk and their perseverance led to the accumulation of wealth

I didn't blindly follow my parent's mantra, instead I followed my dreams to work in different areas and I understood the value of money. My failures and success made me to write this book. Incomes may not be regular; there will be ups and downs in every human life.

My dad got a lot of money from reselling the pianos, he invested that money in bank which was used as long term savings and sometimes used for daily expenses. He didn't make any investment that he didn't wanted and he didn't spend the money he didn't have (borrowing money)

Saving was a habit for my dad from his early days. Poverty has given him a good lesson to learn and he gave that to me. He spent money wisely and used to pay money to the charity also. Saving is the byproduct of getting cash. There is no other quick way to save money.

Never spend all of the money you got from gambling or shares or rents or gifts or work , the first step is to deposit a part of it to savings and spend the rest.

Managing money is one of the things where people have to struggle hard. Some people retire with no money to pay for rent and hospital bills. Some people lose their job and don't know how to maintain their expenses. There is a necessity now to maintain your bank balances for a peaceful future to you and your family. Always keep an alternate plan which will work when the business or job fails. This book would help you achieving the same.

Money Management Benefits

Maintaining a budget plan is an important skill to develop for anyone. Money gives freedom financially. We work eight to fourteen hours a day but we don't take care of the money we earn. Proper care must be taken to save the money for your family and yourself. It is really important to take steps when you are young for your financial success in the near future Benefits of money management is amazing, you need to change the way you think. Winners think things differently; they don't do the things in a normal way like others, instead they do it differently.

Peace of mind

One important benefit of money management is it helps you to maintain a peace of mind, free from tensions. When you knew about the money management techniques, you can now be confident and you can sense the pride of helping yourself and your family. The benefits of money management are endless. When you become an adult or when you are in college, it is really important to know to save money and earn money.

Quality of living

When you know to manage money effectively, it gives you peace of mind and also saves much of your time. You can spend enough time with your family. You will feel happy when everything is under control and you would worry less about your financial needs. So plan accordingly with your future goals. Make time for your family members and it would improve the quality of your living and time.

This MUST STOP Now

You will not accumulate your debs that you can't manage; you will learn more about money managing. Find new ways to save money and find read more often about finances. Debts are scary sometimes because they can consume all your income and stop you from achieving your goals. So it is necessary to pay off your debts on time and stop it from exceeding its limits. Plan ahead and work accordingly to make your goals come true. Never overdraw from the bank account and never spend over limit on your credit card.

NO MORE Paycheck to Paycheck

Paychecks to paycheck are big headaches. Every month your expenses are exceeding your income. You earn more money but you don't know to manage money properly. Use your money resourcefully and track your spending patterns. Make a plan for the monthly expenses; do not invest in more money on anything that you can't afford to pay later. This would help you saving from debts and stop you running from paycheck to paycheck.

Analyzing your position

Make a budget plan for the month and follow the same for coming months. You should track the progress of it and make sure you are doing well than the past. You will Analyze where the money goes every month, you could see whether you are spending your money well or just wasting your money. Save the money and add it to your vacation fund or retirement fund. Once you make the analyzing, you could find where you have gone wrong. Take an excel sheet and list down the things you purchase or the sources where you get the income from. This way it will be simple to point out where you have gone wrong and recover from it the next time.

Retirement plan

Save money now and better managing the money helps you in the long run. You can add that money to your retirement plan. Manage your finances for a better retirement for you. When you manage your money well, you help your children in turn by helping them learn good money management skills. They would follow you for a risk free financial success. This would help them earn more money for college or for job. Good money making and money management skills to be followed for the rest of your life.

The Importance of Saving and Budgeting

Creating a budget is the only way and the easiest way to manage your money, set money aside for paying bills and to spend during vacation time or make new investments. Consider your income and expenses, then you will have to analyze how the expense to be lesser than the income. Stick to the budget and make it as habit. You could now be free from all other problems and it is easier. Set your own goal and it would be easier to follow. Make a realistic plan to fulfill your dreams. Create a monthly budget; make a worksheet so that you can keep things in control. Creating a budget is not going to help you solve all your financial needs, unless you work on your goals every day. But it is the first step and important step to do. It improves the financial health and financial stability. Just believe you can do it and you can.

Many people underestimate the risk of overspending and put their families at trouble. On the other hand, some people are wealthy and create quick money in a short period of time. Did you ever wonder how they did it in a short period of time? It is because they have a planning and they have a simple understandable budget to follow. They religiously follow the budget and become successful.

Saving money and spending money is an art, by which you can help yourself and others. You are now a major resource for others around you. This would also help you to achieve your career goals. You can use the money to pay for college and take the college courses you wanted to.

Life is really tough to understand. One day you might get a higher position in job and other day you may fail badly. You will have to take care of your health, which might also cost you more in the future. So, it is good to save for the rainy days for peaceful living. There is no minimum age to start anything new, but following a plan is the key for success.

When you are not married, the expenses are less. But when you get married, your family needs expand. When your kids go to school or college, the demand grows very bad and it would become a nightmare to you.

When you make a plan, with 100$ for food per month and actually the food bills are up to 350$ every time, then it is not going to work. You need to re-structure that plan again and make space by reducing other incomes or making new changes. You have struggled with your financial problems for a long time, you didn't make an improvement. It's now time to change the plan and choose what works for you. There are plenty of ideas to implement, what may work for someone make not work for you, so choose wisely. Excel spreadsheets has been the greatest tool for analyzing the budgets. So sit down and rethink with your partner to reconstruct a new budget for a bright future.

It's hard time Managing Money

Managing money sometimes may be similar to dieting, this would give a long term benefits to you and your family members and would bring an amazing lifestyle change for you. There is much abundance of sources online from books to magazines and articles. Even it gets hard to manage money. What are the factors that stop us from achieving our goals?

More choices

These days there are more choices and more plans to choose in the case of financial needs for you. Consider the life insurance or mutual funds; there are plenty of plans around us. They are confusing to choose. There is no simplicity nowadays, gone are the days with just two choices. Our daily life becomes more complicated and troubled. You are confused with the decision making, you can't clearly think of which plan to choose. It causes disappointment, frustration and finally you give up.

Change in Lifestyle

I am not free, you are not free and everyone is busy with something. We are always occupied with family, work, community, kids and all other works. Mostly we are on the phone all the time, this doesn't give us time to concentrate on money managing. Our hours are simply getting wasted by running on daily household works. You don't have to time to concentrate and you fail having no time to pay checks on time. There should be proper organizing in terms of financial matters, which would improve in the long run.

Media to Blame

Nowadays media are to be blamed for the too much cost of the prices and so much hype. Most TV sitcoms show you to live rich but not telling how to achieve. There is daily bombardment from the TV sitcoms, movies, websites and commercials about the latest things, which in turn drains your money. These media things are emotional. You must be able to keep up with your payments. You aren't aware of the new product and you purchase blindly which spoiled your monthly budget. Media tempt us more to buy the latest product like TV or Laptop which is unnecessary sometimes. This would cause an unexpected expense.

Types of budgets

There are different types of budgets served for different purposes, let us look at the types of budgets. Although it may or may not be suitable for individuals or personal, but overall it is better to know about the type of budgets.

Capital Budgets

This is a long term budget say for 12 months it includes the costs like building, land and furniture, computers etc., it includes the major capital purchases. It may include the budget plans for the next year.

Operating Budgets

It is used in a firm; this is a budget for a particular year and operating currently. It includes the budgets related to production, sales and finished goods. It is actually of two types one is the expense budget and another is the revenue budget. The expenses of a firm are indicated by the expense budget and the incomes related to the firm are shown by the revenue budget for the coming year.

Cash Budgets

All the cash inflows and outflows for a firm are to be collectively included in the cash budget. It includes the cash disbursements, receipts, net change in cash and financing newly. The shortage and overage of cash can be managed here, which is quite useful.

Sales Budgets

The sales that are to be made in a year are indicated by the sales budget. The budget determines the sales potential, it is projection of how much sales a firm can make. It is a control mechanism and planning instrument. Everything indicating to sales is noted here.

Personnel Budgets

Salary and wages are included here in this budget. The costs to the labors are also indicated here. The recruitment costs, training, hiring, overtime costs and discharge are explained here. The number of staff and staffing ratios are included too. So this explains the personnel budgets.

Budgets for individual

Cost saving budget

This budget is for people to save money on a monthly basis. You can save the money for a particular year and would be easy. This budget is making quick steps ahead of the time. Like the winter clothes are cheaper in the summer, you can buy the clothes ahead and save more money. This helps to save the cost of the product and get the better quality of product. Buying combo products is another option; you could save some money on them.

Problem solving budget

This is the second budget we discuss and more useful one. This step helps you identify the problematic areas. When you avoid more problems, you are easy to achieve your goals. Buy what you want really buy, some purchases can be made at a later time. Once you identify these two areas, you will get more time to concentrate on other things.

Planning budget

Allotting the floating money to the categories is the important step to be followed. Suppose when you want to make a family tour trip, you can use this money for your needs. This money can be used in the case of hospital emergency or other quick expenses. This is the type of budget you need to follow.

Step Budget Making Process

Reduce your hectic schedules, unsatisfied things and more things discussed before. It is the time to concentrate on the important financial decisions and being productive. There is a lack of proper information when it comes to debt managing and spending. Analyze the steps; make time and energy to learn the new things. Determine what would work for you in the future and follow the steps to get started.

List the priorities

After the 9/11, everyone feared about the financial status and other issues. It is better to list out the top priorities and ignore all others. Re-create your list; make the effort to complete on time on a regular basis and make a proper schedule to analyze and re sketch the plans.

Choose the system

There are many money management techniques already available in the market. So recreating them is highly risk and research on them is purely to be avoided. It is better to choose one method and follow the same. It takes long practice to save money. So, pick one system and move on with the same, it would benefit you in the long run.

Traditional or computer

If you are not used with computer, you can still stick to the pen and paper. It is more traditional and easier. Computer make cause eye strain when staring it for 8 to 10 hours. Better you can download some apps to help you or download workbooks. We will look about budget apps in other section. This would save you thousands of dollars in the long run and you would know where the money is going. You can create your own excel sheet in my opinion, it will be good for your needs rather than downloading the workbook from online. Or you can download the workbook and make the changes to them in your own style. So keep motivated and stick to it.

Converse with your family members

Make a routine every week to analyze the problem of managing the expenses with your family members. Make decisions ahead of the time, stay with the current trends to save money and live better. Talking with them about your problems may give you a bit of relief and help you analyze things better. Make things smarter, you can automatically pay your bills through the bank account you hold and make sure to pay the credit bills on time. This will save your time and money for a better future.

Figure out what you are worth

After you have determined your goal, the next step is to analyze the current financial situation. How much are you worth in terms of money and you needed to know how to accomplish your goal? The worth I mentioned here is comprised of savings and other assets. Savings are your deposits in the bank and others which you can easily turn in to cash. Most assets are holdings which cannot be easily changed into cash easily. It is jewelry or real estate or used TV. If you can analyze your current position correctly then you can make an effort to reach your goal.

Make note of your financial goals

Making note of your financial goals is the first step to do. Analyze your goals; make a list of goals you want to achieve which includes repaying the debts, building savings. Think about your short term and long term goals and start to achieve them. Write them down somewhere and you can achieve them easily.

Record every single purchase

Make a habit to record every single purchase you make, the every expense you make from your pocket helps to be alert on the spending in a particular month. You never knew that you spent so much money on food or clothing. Knowing your spending habits is one way to get back on track.

Top Budgeting Apps

These days there are apps to save your time. Whether you are in debt or saving money for a specific goal, you can try the budget apps which help you to reach your financial goals. Listed below are some of the top apps.

Personal Finance

This is the app that received so much acclaim due to the easy controls and saving time. Mint.com apps connect to all of your accounts immediately and you can check the net position quickly. You can categorize your spending, check balances, pay bills and check your budget. You can set reminders for low account balance and upcoming payments notifications. You can sync your laptop, android phone and tablet, which can be later, changed and remove from the settings if you lose them. It is free and available with iTunes and Google play store.

Easy Envelope Budget Aid

This is a high end app that is used for tracking your regular and irregular expenses. You record your spending and the app maintains the total. You can every time check the balance before spending. There is no need of adding your bank accounts and make it risk. The data is stored online and there is fear of data loss, you can get back the data whenever you want. The app is synced with all devices, so you can maintain it easily. It is available free from iTunes and Google play store.

Good Budget

This app is formerly called as EEBA; this is great app to start with which is based on cash flow. The money can be allocated and put into envelopes similar to actual envelopes every month which is old fashioned and easy. You can understand the spending habits in every area of your life. The timeframes can be changed accordingly to every month or week or monthly or every two weeks. You can also track at irregular times when the spending is not routine. This is a free app, available for both android and IOS devices.

Mvelopes

The app starts with few questions about your financial goals. You can sync up your bank accounts, which are very secure. It is not for short term and doesn't work like a financial planner or advisor but it guides you about money. You can sync many bank accounts after several rounds of email confirmations. It works directly with the financial institution tracking every credit and debit transactions just like Mvelopes.

After the syncing process, it functions much similar to GoodBudget. It uses the envelope system and you need to define the income and a fixed budget has to be allotted before spending the same. This way you get to know who much money you have in your account and the reasonable budget you maintain for the same. You are now spending the money on your budget rather than the actual net income. This is a free app available for Android and IOS.

Bill Guard

Bill Guard is the new budget app, which helps you understand your spending habit and protects you from unauthorized transactions. First you need to sync your bank account, after you had done that. You can quickly see your total balance and amount you have spent this month. The goals set by the app are correct and true to the needs of the users.

Swipe right if you made a transaction and swipe left if you didn't make it. It stays there actually. Your inbox would show emails when you have made transactions. If you swipe left, the pop up screen appears with the following (Help me, report/contact, follow up later)

Choose the last option, when you don't have time or busy at the moment. After you had made any transaction. You can see in the all tab and the transactions listed with merchant name, type of purchase, date, amount spent. This app is free for Android and IOS.

Pocket Expense

This app gives you a visual outlook on your spending and you can track your spending. You can create your fixed budget. This app however does not sync with the bank accounts, you should manually enter all the transactions. You can check your savings and enter how much you want to spend from there. The credit numbers are shown in green, while the debts and expenses are shown in red. You can also add multiple accounts and check them quickly. You can look the expenses per day, per week, month or any time. This way you can check your spending breakdown. This app is free and can be downloaded for Android and IOS.

Home Budget

This app is superb; it is clear and easy to navigate. The home screen displays the dollar amounts, accounts, budget, income and expenses. The expenses are displayed as a percentage of income with total balance and color coded, which is easy to understand. This app is easy to navigate unlike the other apps. Payees search and reports are the three tabs you could see at the end of the screen.

This is much helpful for the freelancers by entering the client name along with the date or description. You can look at the reports table if you want further information. You can check month to month spending, accounts and budgeting. If some people are paying your regularly you can add them to the payees section. The search option in the app is truly amazing, you can quick search something whether it is a check or a client you forgot the details of the same. Just search the client name and you will get a pop up message. There are two versions of this app for android and IOS. The elite version is free and the IOS version is 5.99$

Budgeting Rules

The budgeting rules that we will discuss here is simple and easy to keep in mind. You need to allocate 50 percent of the money to your basic needs i.e., food, shelter and clothing. Also medical needs and gym are to be included here.

Save the 20 percent of your monthly income regularly. You can use it for retirement plans, for repaying the loans that you have taken before or put it in the emergency fund for later. Keep the money other than this separately; you can also allocate 30 percent of your money for day to day expenses. You can use it for your internet bills, food etc.

When you are paid a salary, 25 percent of the salary goes as tax. You are left with 75 percent of total money. Use the first 25 % to the housing loans or building needs. Remember that shelter is the first priority. Use the next 25 % to the debts; make it to repay your debts on regular basis. Remaining 25% you can use it for daily expenses or save it for emergency fund.

Steps to follow when making a budget for an irregular income earner

The life of a freelancer or someone with irregular income can be very tough. He or she needs to be making a hand to mouth existence. There is no other way for them to be like a rich person or someone who is employed with a constant job. And budgeting process would be a nightmare for them. I will list down three simple steps to follow for an irregular income earner.

Separate bank account

One way to make a budget is to open a separate bank account. Use one account to receive the checks. The checks could be from any time in the week. Just pay the checks in the bank account. You will have another account for frequent money withdrawing for your expenses. You have to make it as habit to transfer the funds to another every week. This would be regular habit to follow.

List the priorities

We have already discussed this step before, list down the priorities that are really important for you at this moment. Sometimes you feel like you want to take a course, you can however take it at a later stage also. This would save your money and your time. Converse with your partner to make the financial decision and it will work out for you.

MIMIC the paycheck

Sometimes it would be really tough and you might not be in a position to manage funds. In that situation, it is better to have hope and follow. You have to be positive and mimic the paycheck. The lowest amount you got is your starting point and you have to manage your funds from there. You have to work out hard to make things possible.

Controlling expenses and how to spend less

There are several steps to control your expenses and spend less money. Some of the tips are simple and would amaze you a lot. It can be followed by anyone and helpful in the long run. Let us look at the steps one by one.

Combo pack

When you need to spend money on cable TV, phone bills and Internet every month, there is an easy way to manage all these. Opt for the combo pack, these packs are easy and you save more money by combining the packs. The service providers offer 3 services at the cost of one. The discounted fee is less comparing to the original cost.

Maintaining good health

Maintaining good health can save your time and money. Being fit is a good habit to develop. You don't need to hit the gym and do the pushups. You can start small by walking daily or climbing the stairs. This is a simple exercise to do and can help you in the long run. This way you save a lot of money on health care. You don't need to buy equipment which is too costly. You can stay with skipping rope or stretching wheel.

Revise your car insurance plans

Every year make sure to revise your car insurance plans. There are different car insurance plans to choose from. So go through all the car insurance plans once and make a best choice. You can figure out easily with the less cost and more options. This job is not a hard; you can do it easily online too. This would save your money and you don't need to pay penalties.

Maintaining the credit score

Do maintain the credit score every time below 0.50% and it would help you in the long run. You will save fortune. This includes the car insurance, home loans, credit cards etc. This will also be stress free and simple to follow. Keep in mind to maintain below the 50 points.

Don't use overdraft

If you are debit card holder and you often use the debit cards, then don't go for the overdraft facility. It will make you addicted to more spending and at the end; it will become a big burden. Don't spend too much and don't buy things which you can't afford to repay. These figures would become a nightmare at the end of the year.

Use internet shopping

Online shopping is the easiest and the simplest way to shop products. You can now shop at the ease of your home and no work needed. The most online shopping portals provide huge discounts which will be helpful to buy more things and less work for you. But choose the better cost and better quality before making a decision.

Make short term targets

Make a plan to save a particular amount of money in a short period of time. This way you can achieve your targets and you can be free from financial troubles in short period of time. Make small targets and easy to achieve, big targets are hard and boring. It is better to start with small amounts initially and move on to bigger amounts.

Be a better cook

Instead of buying expensive cakes and chocolates, why can't you try your favorite food at home? This way you can save a lot of money and eat quality food at home. Most shopping outlets will sell you unhealthy junk foods. It is good to make your choice to cook on your own of the favorite recipes you like.

21 day rule

If you want to start something new, it has to be easy and simple to understand and mostly you should be able to make it as a habit. For any new thing to become a habit, you will have to religiously follow for 21 days. And later it becomes a practice. You can also analyze about yourself about the faults you make. This way it will be a short review and become a habit.

Ways to make extra money

1. Become a blogger. One way to make quick bucks to become a blogger, you can write about the favorite things and you can get paid easily.

2. Teaching. You can coach other people on what you are good at. You can be a yoga teacher or swimming coach. You can help other people with languages and you can get paid more.

3. Learn Photoshop. These days' logos are of huge demand and you can make money easily by making a logo and get paid.

4. Stock trading. You can get rich by trading stocks at your own comfort. Learn more about stock trading and you can get rich quick.

5. Online store. You can setup an online store, which can help you in many ways. You can shop and sell on eBay, Amazon or any other market giants.

6. Rent vehicles. You can rent your car or van to get an income. understand this is not your main profession , but you can do it as a hobby and get paid

7. Learn music. By learning music you can earn money easily. You can go the church and pay piano there during weekends.

8. Marketing .you can market different products either online or directly to people. This would save a lot of money.

9. Rent buildings .you can rent your own buildings and get some income every month. This is a best passive income to make.

Budgeting and Debt Management

Debt management (particularly unsecured) is the first venture to taking control of your cash! Include a family planning arrangement and you've got an effective apparatus for cash management. Together, planning and debt management construct budgetary security and autonomy. Yes, you can decrease debt and put something aside for your future monetary security in the meantime! It could be possible.

Anybody can do it and everybody merits it!

Actually, it's the main planning arrangement that bodes well. Planning to incorporate debt management in your own FINANCE arrangement assembles a decent solid protection against credit card utilization. Startling occasions and costs assume a huge part in making debt for the majority of us. A decent planning arrangement that sets you up for those occasions and gives a solid establishment to fall back on is key for fruitful debt management.

This is the place most made toward oneself financial plans come up short. Indeed, even the best propositions are bound on the off chance that you will be you blameworthy of this normal oversight? Without a complete arrangement, we fall right once again into the old credit card trap. Feeling powerless and cornered into utilizing credit to simply bring home the bacon. Free yourself from the weight of credit card debt. You will never be monetarily autonomous the length of you need to rely on upon the credit card organizations to survive.

Stopped putting resources into the credit card organizations and begin putting resources into you! Yes, I know the emotions great. Scarcely making a decent living, planning disorder, attempting to keep up "everything's O.K." while finances keep on deteriorating and more terrible. Stop the sentiments of insufficiency and disappointment! In today's quick moving society it's not abnormal for the normal family to be living way past their methods. Considering that, quit faulting yourself. This is the world we live in. Society's desires have caught a large portion of us.

I settled on the choice to stop the frenzy and help myself! You can as well! A planning arrangement that incorporates overseeing debt will help you succeed at cash management. Make an arrangement taking into account your individual needs...set your own goals...and start your voyage to long lasting monetary security and freedom! Truth be told, we all have distinctive needs and commitments, so everybody's arrangement must be intended to suit their interesting circumstance.

The way to budgetary achievement is to live inside your methods!

The way to free riches is living beneath your methods! Anyhow wait…we're stretching way beyond now. In the wake of living way past your methods for so long, it's sufficiently hard to accept this reality. When you have that aced, and perceive the amount of cash you didn't even know you had, you'll be energetic to scale down considerably more! Debt management is critical for any planning arrangement to succeed. What's more, moreover, a great family unit planning arrangement is vital for any debt management project to succeed. One can't be fruitful without the other. Like "peanut spread and jam" the vast majority of us can't have one without the other. They simply go together!

Care giving and Money Management

Dealing with cash matters can be baffling, overpowering, and even unnerving for senior natives. Numerous individuals, including my grandma, often go to the client administration office at their bank for help adjusting their checkbooks. This is a decent arrangement, yet there are other simpler approaches to keep away from issues. On the off chance that you have an in home parental figure that has the capacity help with finances, the senior resident can evade the frightfulness that rises up out of missing cash and in the meantime, dodge an additional outing out to the bank.

Extraordinary cash management aptitudes are essential for this errand. Most seniors are on a settled wage, either singularly Social Security advantages, or maybe a benefits or an annuity payout notwithstanding Social Security. In any case, a financial plan is a need. Assessing the amount of cash is coming in and contrasting that number with the amount of is going out in costs is a decent place to start. The most ideal approach to start with this is by beginning with unquestionably the fundamental costs. Take their month-to-month salary and subtract these costs off the top. This incorporates rent/home loan expenses, basic needs, service bills, and any prescription or doctors visit expenses that exist. After this, the remaining cash can be utilized for more optional purposes. Diversion ought to likewise be considered-everybody needs to have a ton of fun and unwind sooner or later amid the day. This may come as a link bill, books, magazine memberships, or actually putting resources into a feature amusement framework. In all trustworthiness, it doesn't make a difference what they accomplish for entertainment only; the length of they are having a great time and not lounging around in fatigue, stimulation is a decent cost.

More than great cash management abilities are important when managing a senior native's finances. You have to be dependable and proficient also. No one needs to turn over his or her own finances to a more bizarre, so you have to be as mitigating as would be prudent when managing a senior. Keep in mind that there is a solid human component in this kind of errand. Yes, you are assisting with finances, yet you are managing an individual's finances. Remember this.

A discretionary errand that a cash administrator may experience is giving trusts to arrangements. Verifying that there is sufficient cash accessible in their financial records may be a piece of your obligations too. As a parental figure, you have to guarantee that the senior you are administering to has the proper restorative help. On the off chance that they are not able to plan for specialist copayments, you will rapidly run into issues. Adjusting checkbooks appropriately and keeping up the perfect measure of cash in their financial records will be a flat out need for giving your customer the consideration that they fancy.

Teens and Money Management

From CD's to mobile phones to films with their companions, youngsters have a method for depleting your pockets. Instructing youngsters at early stage cash management aptitudes will without a doubt pay off over the long haul.

Don't simply give your adolescents a stipend; show them to win it by meeting expectations, i.e. doing errands. Show them to spare cash, by opening an investment account and saving a bit of their stipend every week. It is critical to make manages on how regularly they can make withdrawals. Have them keep a log of the amount they spend and what they spend it on. This won't just reveal to them what they are squandering cash on, however it will permit you to keep tabs too.

More established

"A few kids get as much as $50 week pocket cash… However research shows teenager way of life expenses a bundle." The study demonstrated that more seasoned high scholars' are procuring a normal of $245 every week—A mix of working, pocket cash, errands, and/or cash blessings got.

As teenagers get more seasoned and start working, this is not motivation to negligence the standards of cash management. They ought to still be obliged to put a part into their investment account and they ought to still be considered responsible for their spending. This may be a tricky subject and, "It's my cash," is certain to come up, yet tenets are standards, and you must stick to them.

ON THE SAME PAGE

It is critical that everybody cooperate. On the off chance that you have a life partner, you must be in concurrence with the course of action. On the off chance that one guardian gives in, it doesn't advantage anybody. There is nobody brisk fix to tackling monetary issues, however the best technique is avoidance. Showing your youngsters cash management abilities will tell them from the get-go that they need to work for things that they need, that they must spare cash, and that they ought to spend their cash admirably.

TIPS AND IDEAS

Here are a couple of tips that will help you make a blueprint for your youngster:

Make a reasonable plan and stick to it. In the event that you have more youthful youngsters, alter their recompense, as they get more seasoned. On the off chance that the errands have not been finished, don't be hesitant to not issue them remittance for the week. DON'T BUY ON IMPULSE. Don't get sucked into the "Kindly if its not too much trouble please I got to have it," line.

On the off chance that you have a more seasoned youngster, consider issuing them a money card rather than money. You can stack their stipend onto the card and they can utilize it at stores, or make withdraws at an ATM machine. Toward the end of the month, you can take a seat and audit the buys made. Verify that a part of that goes into their bank account. Consider giving your youngster a "reward" for doing great in school or tackling additional errands. This will demonstrate to them that you can be compensating for doing great. Taking the time to educate your youngster's great cash management will presumably be one of the best interests in time you will ever make. These lessons will set up your youngsters with the abilities to secure a decent budgetary future.

Money Management For Couples

First among the reasons that prompt relational conflicts are often issues with money and finances. Most couples are not able to or discover it to a great degree hard to suggest the subject straightforwardly and sincerely. Despite the facts that the reasons may be diverse for every couple, being confused and not able to convey are regular.

So as to keep away from genuine outcomes it is important to for couples to actualize the craft of planning and cash management. Couples ought to keep away from clash over buys made by one another and figure out how to regard one another's assessments.

The beginning step is to take a seat and talk about the wage and consumption. In the event that there is an absence of correspondence, which is the situation more often than not, this examination could end in a warmed contention. It is vital to settle on a system before hand, to keep a monstrous circumstance. For instance, get up and drink a glass of water, take a couple of full breaths and strive for a short walk and after that resume the dialog or welcome a companion to be a piece of the exchange. Make a rundown of every last one of charges that are pending and the sums, highlighting the dates on which they have to be paid. Contrast this and the joint pay and in the event of insufficient trusts, attempt to discover approaches to decrease consumption or build pay.

Report all statistical data points with the goal that they are effortlessly accessible to your accomplice. Make a different document for records and papers identified with protection installments, credit card proclamations, auto portions, month-to-month contract, service bills and costs. Expel them from the record just when they are paid. Choose a typical spot open to both, to keep checkbooks, receipts and all significant money related data. In the event that there have been withdrawals from the shared service, every accomplice ought to tell the other the reason.

Such dialogs ought to be planned consistently. Monetary arranging ought to be a key piece of the talks. Money related issues get to be distressing if not maneuvered carefully. Make an arrangement to guarantee that both of you alternate to look after checkbooks, document charges and track speculations. This will permit every accomplice to be mindful of the budgetary subtle elements. Talk about and make a financial plan to suit both of you.

Attempt to picture finances for the following five or ten years. A lot of cash are needed for purchasing a house or another auto.

The distinctive courses in which you could put something aside for these buys ought to be talked about transparently.

When you set your objectives, devise a technique to accomplish them. The arrangements would chiefly involve wiping out debt and setting up a funds arrangement. One astounding way would be to spare a certain rate of the month to month pay in an assessment conceded record. You can likewise spare and put resources into securities and bonds.

Budgetary mismanagement is for the most part a key considers destroying an upbeat marriage. With a specific end goal to keep finances more right than wrong, fitting correspondence is vital. Consistent dialogs and common choices on the family plan and funds are certain approaches to keep up the congruity among couples.

Credit Counseling and Debt Management Programs

Not all credit directing administrations oblige that customers take an interest in a debt management program, and not all shoppers who need credit advising likewise oblige a debt management program. A debt management system is a program that helps shoppers with their current debt. Qualified credit instructors will investigate your debt and wage levels, examine alternatives for escaping from debt, and talk about the favorable circumstances and drawbacks of a debt management program with you.

In the event that it is dead set that a debt management project is the proper arrangement of activity for your circumstance, the credit guide will add to an installment plan with each of your unsecured creditors, trying to bring down the aggregate sum of cash owed, diminish your advantage rates, and have over the point of confinement and late expenses expelled from records while you are taking part in the credit guiding debt management program.

How Debt Management Programs Work

When you join a debt management program, you will start making a regularly scheduled installment to the credit guiding organization. The organization then takes those stores and uses them to make installments for your benefit to your understudy credits, CREDIT CARDS, hospital expenses and other unsecured debts- utilizing the installment plan that the credit guide has worked out with your creditors.

It's generally a smart thought to get the debt management system terms in composing and afterward inquire as to whether they really do offer the concessions that the credit advocate has demonstrated.

Effective debt management projects may take 2 years or more to pay off your debt. Your credit advocate ought to have the capacity to gauge to what extent it will take you to totally pay off each of your current debt, and chances are you will be needed not to seek or utilize whatever other credit while you are a piece of the system.

Things to ask before Enrolling in a Debt Management Program:

Before marking an agreement or making a promise to utilize a debt management program, there are more inquiries you ought to request that in place figure out whether the debt management project is the best choice for your circumstance.

On the off chance that a credit directing office just offers debt management programs as their administration, you ought to most likely think about utilizing as an alternate credit advising program that can likewise give help planning and cash management.

Ask how the regularly scheduled installment is resolved. On the off chance that the debt management installment is higher than what you can manage the cost of every month- you're not going to make any advancement by utilizing the system. Verify the regularly scheduled installment is sufficiently sensible that you can make the installment as obliged every month prior to the due date.

Discover how the debt management project makes installments to creditors. Will it be inside the charging cycle and before the due date? Do they make regularly scheduled installments to creditors or would they say they are on some other timetable? How does their installment calendar influence your debt?

Are there any debts that you presently have that can't be incorporated in the debt management program? Figure out why, and verify that you can bear to pay that bill all alone while as yet paying the proposed debt management regularly scheduled installment.

Ask the credit advisor how the debt management project will influence your credit. On the off chance that they let you know they can evacuate negative checks on your credit report, they're off-base. Legitimately, just off base negative stamps on your credit history can be uprooted before the seven year period is over.

Verify the project you are considering is a debt management program and not a debt transaction arrange as they are two altogether different techniques, and a debt arrangement can have dependable negative results for your credit report.

Obliterate Debt has the counsel and assets you require on debt combining and other budgetary themes.

Parents Should Pass on Effective Money Management Skills to Their Kids

Each minding guardian needs to have the capacity to give the world to their children and do all in their energy to verify they are situated on a course for an extraordinary life all around. One of the best and most imperative things a guardian can do that will be tremendously useful to their youngsters at each phase of their lives is to issue them cash management tips and show them sound cash management standards.

Regularly, when people attempt to give their children a decent youth loaded with the greater part of the heavenly, instructive and fascinating toys and recreations that are famous, it can really blowback as far as showing youngsters obligation with cash. Amid the developmental years, if youngsters are regularly given $20 toys without comprehension individual FINANCE cash management, soon their "toys" transform into $20,000 autos when they achieve adulthood.

There are numerous people who appear to be willing and just about energetic to bail their posterity out with the different money related difficulties and emergencies that they experience, even far into their grown-up years. Be that as it may, these well intentioned people additionally need to make careful arrangements to make certain that they don't overextend themselves and wind up bringing about money related issues and anxiety for themselves and that they get ready for fitting cash management to help them through their retirement years.

People can help their youngsters find out about individual budgetary objectives and cash management standards whenever. While it is constantly best to begin right on time in life to find out about dealing with their FINANCES, about how to organize their buys, how to adjust their needs versus their needs, and how to stay inside their financial plans, these are every single money related idea that individuals can find out about any point in time. People who are excessively tolerant from the get-go and who rich an excess of blessings and goodies on their young kids can at present get things back on course by essentially saying no when the solicitations proceed past the age when they ought to stop.

While it can be troublesome, and even traumatic for both the guardian and the kid, when a guardian begins putting points of confinement on the money related help they will offer to their kids, over the long haul it is best for both sides. The posterity will pick up a feeling of confidence and self-assurance as they consider their own money related management important and start to handle their own particular monetary crises, and also their own particular budgetary indulgences toward one's self.

In the meantime, people will feel that their kids will have the capacity to get along without them long after they are gone. They won't be agonizing over how on the planet their descendants will manage finances as they themselves move toward the retirement years. Beginning a cash management arrange early is dependably the best approach, however it is never past the point where it is possible to learn individual budgetary management standards and aptitudes.

How To Manage Your Finances Properly And Improve Your Lifestyle- Money Management

Whether you are dealing with your cash at home or dealing with the cash going into and out of a business, we all realize that this can be disappointing and now and again greatly troublesome. The vast majority battle to pay their bills and, as the expression goes, 'to make a decent living.' All the greater part of us need is to have the capacity to deal with our finances legitimately and to attempt and enhance our ways of life. Cash Management at Home–Understanding finances and dealing with your cash at home need not be troublesome. There is an abundance of learning accessible on the web concerning cash issues so you can settle on the right decisions when arranging your finances. Seeing how home loans and credit work, and how to abstain from incurring some significant debt are critical ranges to address, so that your cash does not oversee you–you have to deal with your cash! There are numerous sites that offer help by giving free on-line plan organizers and plan mini-computers.

Get your work done before utilizing these sites as there could be security issues when inputting record information. These locales are infrequently not dependable either and miscount plans and frequently have bugs as well. Usually, by paying for an on-line plan organizer, you will get far superior programming which will empower you to effectively deal with your bank and credit card records and individual finances. You will likewise get far reaching help and backing in addition to numerous additional administrations that the free destinations don't offer. Clients of these online plan organizers and plan mini-computers will have the capacity to view their records, run reports about their spending and sparing propensities, and deliver clear diagrams and pie graphs which demonstrate their use by class so they can see where their cash is going. The greater part of the distinctive highlights accessible will empower clients to keep focused of their everyday finances and plan and remain focused.

Cash Management in Business–The primary need for any entrepreneur is right cash management. At the point when beginning up another business, the fundamentals from the start is vital, for instance setting up a business ledger, accounting (DIY or utilize a bookkeeper) and how installments will be acknowledged in addition to the credit terms. On the off chance that you decide to deal with your cash yourself, there are various programming alternatives accessible on the web to help with cash management, income, plans and accounting.

Picking the right bundle to suit your specific business needs is essential. A large portion of these projects will permit clients to stay informed regarding the cash coming in and the cash going out (income), make receipts, and to stay informed concerning records payable and receivable and those terrifically critical ledger offsets. Picking the Right Money Management Software–When picking a cash management item, you have to choose what item is best for your necessities. On the off chance that you basically need to stay informed concerning your costs, or need to get back on top of finances that have escaped from control, get your work done before acquiring programming on the web. Cash management can be so natural, and with the right programming you can plan, plan and even put something aside for a superior without debt future!

Money Management Tips to Avoid Bankruptcy

In case you're similar to numerous Americans today, you may discover the greater part of the news encompassing insolvency to be fairly disturbing. In the event that you partake in this assumption, your alert is defended. Liquidation is a trendy expression that is seen progressively frequently in our way of life, and you need to do whatever it takes to keep it from being a word connected to your life.

Keeping away from insolvency is made conceivable with a couple of strong cash management aptitudes. When you begin honing these methods as a piece of your propensity–and urge your family to do as such, as well–you'll almost certainly fight off the liquidation courts the length of you live!

Planning

Planning is the granddad practice of all things that take after. When you make and take after a decent plan, you and your family will create fundamental cash management abilities to administer the majority of your money related choices. A financial plan is similar to your family's Constitution. It figures out what is reasonable, and what is most certainly not. It is interested in change and conformity, however it doesn't change effectively. Modifying your financial plan ought to oblige a considerable measure of discussion and trained thought.

Anyway, in what capacity would it be advisable for you to make a financial plan? On the off chance that you don't recognize what you're spending as of now, begin staying informed concerning the figures. Watch where each penny goes, record it, and perceive how your cash streams. Do this for a month so you can get a decent handle on the greater part of your costs. At that point, make a financial plan that is based off of these perceptions.

You'll likely find you're spending excessively in a few classes, and perhaps you're actually spending too little in others! When you have your financial plan, great cash management practices will just take after in the event that you stick to your financial plan. Numerous individuals helpfully disregard this second piece of the practice a couple of weeks into their new plan! Keep in mind, and you can help avert liquidation!

Crisis Plan

Next step is to make a crisis arrangement (or a secret stash). We can't stretch how crucial this practice is. This store ought to have enough to cover around three months' living costs for your crew. Likewise, sufficiently incorporate to meet your protection arrangement's deductible for all relatives. In the event that you encounter extreme sickness or get to be all of a sudden unemployed, having a crisis arrangement could be what spares your gang. Not having one can put you at a high hazard for liquidation.

We would rather not solid like we're lecturing a fate and-unhappiness message, however a decent crisis arrangement can improve things greatly concerning your family's wellbeing. A decent cash management tip: keep this cash effectively open (i.e. money), and don't give it a chance to twofold for some other reason!

We these two practices, you're well on your approach to having solid cash management abilities. Keep doing awesome, be prepared for putting some sparing and INVESTING aptitudes to utilize!

Budgeting and Cash Management

Planning or monetary arranging includes evaluating the measure of wage and the costs of the impending budgetary year. This is vital in that it helps in the management of products. It has the capacity make an endeavor to comprehend what it can and cannot have the capacity to do together with its accomplishments in the meantime.

The monetary allowance ought to be in a position to demonstrate the objectives and needs of the association. This empowers long haul arranging which will empower the association accomplish its objectives. Keeping in mind the end goal to have the capacity to focus all the costs and the pay got the budgetary reports and records ought to be submitted to the FINANCE board of trustees at constantly. The advisory group ought not depend upon the verbal reports of the supervisor, bookkeeper or the clerk as the primary wellspring of money related data.

All the wellsprings of wage to the business substance ought to occasionally deliver pay and costs plan to the panel. On the off chance that examinations show different commitments cap are past due then their installment arrangement ought to be fused in the monetary allowance. All the costs and salaries ought to be planned for conservatively and sensibly. Any extra subsidizes ought to be set aside to cook for future needs that the association may confront. It might be on operational consumption or repair/capital use.

On the off chance that the element is a school then the FINANCE advisory group ought to be having all the duplicates of the entire plan of the school. This serves to focus the measure of cash that the school needs and the measure of cash it can have the capacity to get from its sources. After the FINANCE board has experienced all the projections of salary and the financial plans from all the different offices and the association ought to be in a position to add to a financial plan that cooks for everything the needs of the association adequately. On the off chance that the board of trustees cannot be in a position to accomplish this it ought to then think of different choices that will adjust everything the needs of the association. These options may be things like gathering pledges functions, giving enthusiastically, imparting of types of gear in the middle of offices and revaluating the requirement for new supplies.

The financial backing ought to be adjusted between the association's objectives and targets. The monetary exchanging year plan ought to be arranged and affirmed by the finance advisory group who has the last approbation power. The monetary allowance ought to then be at the transfer of every last one of individuals from the association.

Money management planning- This includes the expectation of income and costs month-to-month permitting arranged use to decrease income issues. The association's trade ought to be in for spendable dough equalization with the use of the month. Money of over three months ought to be INVESTED. Bank adjusts on business banks ought not be more than 100,000 as a bigger number of trusts than this are not governmentally protected. Credit trusts are somehow ok for hierarchical or institutional stores. To oversee trade in for money the correct way the organist particle ought to have fitting learning of the associations costs and getting ready for the utilization of cash in the privilege and proper way.

Why Money Management Is Vital To Futures Trading Success

Accomplishment as a prospects dealer is reliant on your capacity to ace method, brain research and cash management. Life as a dealer can be remarkably fruitful, yet it can be just as dangerous, especially while you're figuring out how to speck the i's and cross the ts. It would be an error to stop your normal everyday employment until you've aced the three components of fruitful exchanging. Ace stand out and your absence of information and mastery in both of the other two territories may convey you to the verge of fiasco and topple you over. Keep in mind, dominance and equalization of every one of the three components is key to achievement.

In this article, we'll discuss cash management.

Reveal to Me the Money

Great cash management is basic to accomplishment as a prospects broker. You have to know:

step by step instructions to track your outcomes and gain from them;

- instructions to plan and put aside chance capital;

- instructions to differentiate; and, (as melody goes),

- Realize when to hold, when to overlap and when to leave.

Keep A Track Record

Regardless of how huge or how little the exchange, consistently track your outcomes. Keep an everyday score sheet so you know to the second how a long ways ahead or behind you are. It's crucial data in arranging your next move and choosing the amount of danger you can manage. You ought to likewise keep an everyday exchanging journal that tracks your exchanges as well as the reason behind your choices, business sector elements you weighed, how you responded, even how you felt that day. Intermittently assessing your journal will help you distinguish behavioral examples so you can consistently enhance your system.

Financial plan Your Risk

It's similar to they say in Vegas, don't bet with cash you can't stand to lose. It's the same with fates exchanging. Don't exchange with the rent or basic supply cash. Financial plan a sum you can stand to hazard and stick to your financial plan. Exchanging stores ought to be considered investment–it may work out, it may not. Exchange little and take in your framework before you expand your danger.

Broaden

By broadening, you diminish your danger. In the event that you put all your investments tied up on one place and win, you win enormous; yet in the event that you lose, you lose huge. Partition your speculation between a few choices and nobody move will blow you out of the water. Your wins may be littler yet they'll get to be more reliable and more various. Over the long haul, you'll outpace the competition.

Listen for Alarm Bells

As Kenny Rogers sings in The Gambler: "You got the chance to know when to hold 'em, know when to overlap 'em, know when to leave and know when to run." If you can't leave an exchange when something doesn't appear to be correct, you've got an issue. You need to listen for those inside alerts. Fates exchanging is similar to poker. For the ignorant and unwary, it's a high-stakes session of chance where the likelihood that you'll lose your shirt poses a potential threat. For the shrewd and experienced broker, it's a session of ability, procedure and cash management with the potential for enormous prizes. The trap is in knowing the distinction.

Once you've comprehended the cash management part of fates exchanging, now is the ideal time to proceed onward to procuring the strategies and disguising the brain science vital to achievement in the field.

Top Tips on How to Budget Your Money

Presently like never before is the significance of planning your cash an unquestionable requirement in today's economy. The most imperative thing to recollect when framing your financial plan is disposition. It is basically up to you whether you take after your financial plan or not thusly by having a decent demeanor towards accomplishing your monetary objectives is basic to your prosperity. Planning your cash permits you to set something aside for things that mean something to you. Nonetheless, in the event that you view planning in a negative light its absolutely impossible that you will have the capacity to attain to what you need. Utilizing your demeanor to further advance your objectives through endeavors of sparing and accumulating will empower you accomplish these objectives snappier and simpler. Since you have ingrained your state of mind to implement your capacity to spare you are prepared the right thinking to go ahead with your financial plan.

Since you have had disposition conformity, you must recall to tweak your financial plan to settle your needs and needs. For in the event that you tackle a general methodology you lose all sense of direction in the ideas that others live by rather than your own. For each individual has diverse salaries, bills, and costs so it is extremely unlikely a general plan could work. Be that as it may you can utilize general rules in view of rates for the measure of cash that ought to be dispersed to lease, nourishment, and stimulation. For a financial plan demonstrates to you where you put your significance and permits you to see where additionally financing must be submitted in request to achieve your monetary objectives. On the off chance that you don't have arranged money related objectives it is extremely unlikely you will have the capacity to put something aside for something that is vital to you. Verify that before you begin a financial plan you recognize what course you need to go. Arranged monetary objectives will help to take out drive spending.

Setting up a legitimate plan that is redone to your needs and needs will permit you to see where your cash is going. In seeing the genuine assignment of your cash, you may establish that they way you are carrying on with your life needs a tremendously required conformity. Alternately you may understand that you are so near to your objectives that you may need to change it so you attain to your objectives speedier. Whatever the case may be looking towards what's to come is an extraordinary way to deal with take when attempting to figure out where you need to be not far off. Keeping in mind the end goal to get to where you need to go in life it takes arranging. In setting up a fitting plan you are headed to attaining to the majority of your money related objectives without any difficulty. Verify that you are not relinquishing excessively for you may get to be focused on bringing about your demeanor to slip back where it once was. Sparing cash is an incredible approach to perceive how you have the capacity to deal with your cash with no different unessential variables.

An Essential Tool For Money Management-Budget Planner

It is essential to plan your financial plan, whether individual or for your business.

Individual Budget Planner: In many cases an individual plan organizer ought to cover a time of a year on the grounds that every month is diverse–quarterly bills, yearly protections, auto adjusting and MOT, Christmas and summer occasions.

I would set up my own financial plan on a spreadsheet in light of the fact that it is so easy to change and upgrade. In the event that you incline toward you can download free individual planning programming or purchase a suitable plan organizer bundle. The preference of purchasing a bundle is that most incorporate free bolster and redesigns. To begin with you ought to rundown every one of your costs–include the family, they may consider things that you have neglected, (for example, pocket cash). Bear in mind things, for example, your day-by-day daily paper, which can signify a considerable amount throughout the span of a month.

Begin with costs that happen consistently, for example, home loan, travel expenses, phone, sustenance and so on. At that point go ahead to quarterly and yearly liabilities–you may think that it accommodating to take a gander finally year's bank articulations to refresh your memory. At that point list all the family salary–lamentably this presumably won't take as long! In the event that your salary surpasses your costs–you're a fortunate man! If not, you comprehend what you need to do–expand your salary or decline your costs. You could build your wage by tackling additional work or setting up some online business in your extra time. You could diminish your use by removing a portion of the extravagances–again include the family in this and see what they can think of–something you consider an extravagance may seem vital to your kids. Simply recall, arrange your financial plan and stick to it.

Business Budget Planner: A business plan organizer will typically cover a time of five years or more. This is to consider things, for example, supplanting PC frameworks, programming bundles, organization autos and lavish things of hardware. In business, the monetary allowance organizer is generally consolidated into the management accounts. This is so that real consumption can be contrasted and planned use. The bookkeeper will need to examine any critical varieties between the two and report to the business. The business will then choose if the monetary allowance needs to be adjusted or if spending ought to be carried into line with the financial backing. Most organizations will have an incorporated records framework that accommodates plan section in the Nominal Ledger and lets the business stay informed regarding use in every class.

Financial plan arranging is vital for cash management and forward arranging. Organizations can change their arrangements when fundamental–for example postponing the buy of an expansive bit of apparatus for one more year on the off chance that it is as yet working admirably or expanding the staffing plan on the off chance that they hope to tackle more laborers later on. Most organizations would be not able to capacity without a financial plan organizer–it is a crucial device for an effective business.

Money Management For Financial Comfort

We have all heard the expression "cash management" some time recently, whether it is in promotions or on budgetary instruction fragments in the news. Frankly, numerous individuals are not even totally mindful of their general monetary picture, a great deal less their capacity to procure great aptitudes.

Cash management truly does apply to everybody, from the lowest pay permitted by law specialists to CEOs of billion dollar mixtures. Realize that successful management aptitudes are relevant to each monetary situation possible. It truly does not make a difference the amount of aggregate cash there is to oversee; what is important are the fundamental directing standards of how you handle that cash that you do have.

When you are considering your own budgetary management style, consider whether you truly recognize what you have rather than your debt level. Adding to a reasonable, sensible plan is an absolute necessity when arranging your budgetary future. In the event that that musing is alarming to you, realize that planning just takes some practical judgment skills; don't spend more than you make.

Talking about what you owe, most, if not all, cash management tips will allude to credit card debt and how to keep away from it or possibly understand it. Realize that this is something that can be a financial plan buster. A money related management master realizes that credit cards must be utilized admirably–to manufacture a strong credit record–and never be ill-used.

Additionally, the best cash management includes a framework for funds. You require cash at this time, however never dismiss the way that you are most definitely going to need some later, as well. Great management aptitudes include this recompense for your monetary future. You don't need to spare your whole paycheck, yet you ought to be sparing in any event a bit of something out of every check.

These aptitudes are accordingly a basic part of money related solace. Be very much aware of the amount of cash comes in versus the amount you have going out. Attaining to budgetary management and making it a win is going to include a ton, yet never dismiss your essential objective.

Money Management By Creating A Budget

Cash management is much less demanding to control and comprehend in the event that you make a well thoroughly considered and reasonable plan. How would you know what a reasonable plan resembles? As a matter of first importance, you have to perceive that while it is essential to cut your spending of unimportant things and day by day excursions to the candy machines you ought to still make an area in your financial plan for entertainment only. This will keep you from feeling denied while dealing with your cash, yet once that cash is away for the month your spending will need to stop also. At the point when making a financial plan to deal with your cash you ought to start by recording the majority of your altered month to month costs. This would incorporate your rent or home loan, protection, telephone and Internet bills, electric and whatever else you get a month to month bill for, alongside their sums.

Investigate each of these things on your rundown. While some may be unavoidable, there may be others that you are either paying excessively for every month or can dispense with by and large. An

Money Management

exemplary illustration of this is your telephone bill. Numerous individuals pay an abundant excess for a phone and an area line. On the off chance that you have solid wireless administration in your own particular home and a decent PDA arrangement, drop your home telephone membership. On the off chance that you feel you are paying excessively for cell administration, switch to a prepaid card. You can buy a $20 card and make it extend for the whole month. This will permit you to deal with your cash better. After you effectively investigate your settled month to month costs, take a gander at the amount you are presently spending on variable costs, for example, staple goods, suppers out, gas, link, dress and diversion, for example, films. It is essential that you take a gander at a sensible record of the amount you spend in each of these classifications. This will permit you to make reasonable modification.

Supper out is another of those exemplary samples that can murder cash management endeavors. In the event that you and your accomplice eat out once a week you will spend some place around $200 a month or additionally relying upon how extravagant your taste is. There is nothing off with treating yourself occasionally for extraordinary events like birthdays or commemorations, yet you are tossing your cash out the window in the event that you as often as possible feast out. Set an utmost to the quantity of times you can eat out that will fit agreeably into your financial plan. In the event that you can reasonably stand to eat out once a month, set the date on your schedule and make it an exceptional night.

Cash management abilities start by teaching your financial plan. When you have decided a particular measure of cash you can spend every month in every class of your financial plan make envelopes for every classification and name them. One envelope will be for perishables, one for films, one for gas, and so on. At that point put the definite measure of trade you computed in for cold hard currency your financial plan into the envelopes. This cash will need to last a whole month, so pace yourself. On the off chance that you have EXTRA MONEY left over in one of the envelopes when the end of the month moves around then you can treat yourself to an additional film or fun action, or perhaps spare it. On the off chance that you can take after the financial backing you have set for yourself, you will be well on your approach to having great cash management aptitudes.

Building Strong Money Management Skills

Having incredible cash management aptitudes can represent the moment of truth an individual's future in both the long and the short run. Creating cash management abilities anytime in your life, whether youthful or old, can help you dodge insolvency, as well as carry on with a solid, flourishing money related life.

Planning

It could be said; planning aptitudes are the crux of cash management abilities. A decent plan distributes each segment of your finances, helping you accomplish your monetary objectives with plainly settled strategies. With an altered salary and settled uses, there's no purpose behind your sparing and ways of managing money to ever separate from your financial plan. Obviously, it's not an impeccable world thus this won't be the situation consistently. As wage vacillates and crisis costs happen, nobody can anticipate that you will hold to a financial plan with the most extreme religiosity.

Then again, making a financial plan now can help you stay away from liquidation later on.

After you have made a sensible plan, put aside enough cash to cover three to six months of your planning needs on the off chance that you are not able to work or lose your occupation. Having this cash put aside can issue you a safe wellbeing net, also significant serenity.

Sparing

Decide the amount of cash you need to spare, whether it's in a manager supported 401(k), Roth IRA, government security, or low premium bank account with your bank. Expanding your investment funds between a mixture of these may be profitable for you. Consider your objectives and the opportunities accessible to you, make a reserve funds arrangement, and stick with it. Having funds can be a brilliant fortress against liquidation.

Spending

In terms of burning through, anybody with created cash management abilities will let you know: stick to your financial plan or strive for under plan figures. All sides concur; our nation is in a spending emergency on both individual and legislative levels.

Assume liability for your spending, keep your credit to a base, and stick to the monetary allowance!

Contributing

After you have planned, spared, and spent (inside reason), you can begin contemplating contributing your cash carefully. The most obvious administer in cash management with regards to contributing is to never contribute cash you can't bear to lose. Differentiating your ventures is likewise foremost. With an expanded arrangement of progressive to direct hazard speculations you can MAKE YOUR MONEY WORK FOR YOU. Cash management aptitudes require some investment and practice. In the event that at first you don't succeed, don't be debilitated.

Learn Money Management Tips

Cash management is going to spare you critical measures of cash. In the event that you learn cash management tips you positively will fill your pockets with money. The fortunate thing about figuring out how to spare cash is that you can INVEST astutely and afterward you ought to have the capacity to work less. So what cash management tips are helpful?

Well firstly you ought to get together a financial plan. A financial plan is going to demonstrate to you the amount of cash you spend and the amount of cash you spare. A simple plan is to just record the amount you procure in one section and after that in another segment directly down the amount you spend. This can undoubtedly demonstrate to you the amount you are spending over your pay parcel. At that point you can remove the things that are a bit much in your week after week living costs.

Simply posting everything you spend your cash on is going to demonstrate to you precisely what you are spending your cash on. This is the way to cash management. Distinguishing every individual thing and after that investing the energy to consider whether you really require it. This is a fundamental cash management tips that you ought to learn.

Another cash management tip is to keep your cash in the bank. When you take cash out of your ledger and place it in your wallet you have then even more a shot of spending it. This is a fundamental cash management tip that you can without much of a stretch learn and execute. On the off chance that it is not in your wallet, then you are less inclined to spend it.

Another great cash management tip is to spare a certain sum consistently. At that point put this measure of cash into a term store or a high enthusiasm gaining record. You could likewise INVEST in a few shares or stocks and abandon them in there for the long haul. There are a lot of cash management tips online and you can basically do some brisk exploration to discover what cash management tips are going to suit you and your financial plan.

Money Management Starts With Budgeting

A few individuals are commonly great at cash management. They don't make motivation buys and they find themselves able to put something aside for a blustery day. In any case, with a specific end goal to deal with your cash successfully and put something aside for the future, it is important to advise your cash what to do and you can attain to this by making and keeping up a financial plan.

The more definite you can make your financial plan, the better handle you will have on your finances. For instance, on the off chance that you have an excitement class and incorporate everything from motion picture rentals to supper out, you may need to separate that further so you can see precisely the amount you are spending on every action. A few individuals will have a sustenance classification and afterward separate that further by the amount of is spent at the market and the amount of is spent eating out.

Since sustenance is a significant cost for some individuals, it merits its own classification. Also, this is a territory where numerous individuals have a great deal of space to work with in light of the fact that they observe that they make a considerable measure of motivation buys regarding sustenance. Numerous individuals eat out a few times each week, which can indicate an auto or house installment when you add up to the month's receipts.

Cash management likewise becomes an integral factor when you stop to get espresso while in transit to work. A few individuals who have begun keeping a financial plan following quite a while of halting for espresso and a Danish or whatever they have for breakfast have been dumbfounded at the measure of cash they spend before they ever get the chance to work. While several dollars here and there doesn't appear like much, once you begin including the odds and ends, you will observe that you can regularly dispose of a whole debt from your money related picture just by having your espresso at home.

Actually when you don't offer into paltry or motivation buys, keeping a financial plan keeps you on your toes. You will observe that you search harder for deals and you may even begin to utilize coupons. In the event that you have children, you may tune into which eateries offer free children dinners. It is genuinely stunning the attitude you create when you are effectively occupied with keeping up a solid plan.

To a few individuals, it gets to be very nearly like a diversion where they move themselves to spend less in the present month than they did the earlier month. They begin searching for ways they can spare cash and after that they begin setting objectives and coming to them through the shrewd utilization of cash management.

Effective Money Management

With the current condition of the economy, discovering powerful method for dealing with your stores is amazingly essential. Powerful cash management can help you pay your bills on time, diminish debt installment time, and still consider cash toward the end of every month for the sake of entertainment exercises.

To start with, take a shot at making a financial plan. A financial plan can be made utilizing a straightforward Excel sheet or a planning device, for example, Microsoft Money or Quicken. There are additionally assortments of online devices, for example, Rudder, Thrive, or Mint, all of which offer cash management applications. Incorporate any costs for every month inside the monetary allowance and recall to incorporate the not really evident ones, for example, staple goods, gas, protection, restorative costs, eateries, and even excitement. A large portion of your bills or costs are not adaptable, for example, home loan or auto installments and happen in the meantime every month. These costs are unsurprising simple to plan for. Different costs, for example, perishables and diversion are adaptable—in the occasion a cut-back is required, these adaptable costs are the ones to be cut. When you have a financial plan, stick to it.

Next, deal with building a bank account- Utilizing your financial plan focus the sum you can extra to place in an investment account at the every month. Do this routinely. Everybody ought to have a backup stash and sustaining a bank account is the simplest approach to do as such. Plan to keep no less than three months of living costs in an investment account at all times. This implies that your financial plan times three ought to be the base in your investment account.

On the off chance that, toward the end of every month you understand you have EXTRA MONEY not represented anyplace in the financial backing, utilize that cash to pay down existing debt. Case in point, on the off chance that you allot $100 a month for diversion however just utilize half, utilize the remaining $50 to pay off a current debt. This is an extraordinary approach to reduce the measure of interest you will pay over the long haul and the measure of time you will be paying off your advances or credit card.

Different tips that offer powerful cash managements incorporate paying bills on time to evade any late expenses, paying more than the base or paying twice a month on credit cards to lessen premium, and examination shop to discover the best costs and deals. Limit the utilization of a credit card and once the offset is paid off, attempt to keep it that way and shop for less expensive interest rates. Get environmentally friendly and discover approaches to decrease your service charges every month. Perusing your bank proclamation routinely can keep you educated and your financial balance under control, along these lines disposing of over-draft charges.

For the individuals why should fast buy or have a tendency to make negligible buys, a prepaid charge card or a prepaid credit card may be the arrangement. A significant number of these cards offer planning arrangements that can keep you on track. Case in point, discover a card that does not permit over-draft and utilization it just for buys outside of your commonplace costs. You could put a preset measure of $100 for diversion on the card and once that cash is gone, there can be no more cash spent on amusement for whatever is left of the month.

Toward the end of your first month, assess your spending and your financial plan to figure out whether any progressions need to be made. Remember that surprising costs do happen so having cash in an investment account is a certain flame approach to suit those.

Money Management Software

Dealing with your cash gets to be much simpler on the off chance that you have a product system to record and break down the majority of your budgetary information. These cash administration programming projects can do anything from download every day exchanges from your financial records and other venture records, help you plan and recovery toward long haul and transient objectives, and in addition progressing in the direction of taking out obligation. Here are a few suggestions for cash administration programming and what they can accomplish for you.

The main cash administration instrument which is offered online for a little month to month charge is the administration called Mvelopes. This product is particularly outlined as an individual home planning device. Mvelopes meets expectations correspondingly to the antiquated planning instrument of setting trade in for money diverse envelopes to be utilized for distinctive costs. The main contrasts are that Mvelopes offers virtual envelopes. Like Quicken, Mvelopes downloads exchanges from the majority of your money related records day by day and permits you to order every exchange into particular spending classifications.

At the point when contrasting Mvelopes and Quicken or Microsoft Cash, it is anything but difficult to see the contrasts between the two. Not at all like Quicken, Mvelopes permits you to get to your own financial plan from any PC with Internet access. It additionally tracks all your Visa buys and puts aside cash from each of your envelopes to pay it off every month. This highlight permits you to decrease your obligation in a matter of months. With Mvelopes you can likewise pay up to 15 bills every month online free of charge. They likewise give individual planning honing to keep you on track to achieve your objectives. The month to month cost for Mvelopes is $7.90. They offer a 30 free trial offer.

Another online cash administration programming is GnuCash. This administration is free and uses proficient bookkeeping standards to sort out your funds. Like other cash administration programming projects, GnuCash downloads the greater part of your budgetary data from the majority of your financial balances and speculation accounts. It then offers an examination of your spending and sparing propensities complete with diagrams and pie outlines. This cash administration programming is easy to utilize and comprehend; it's much like utilizing your checkbook register. Another advantage of GnuCash is that you can track both individual and business funds so you don't need to have separate projects for every substance. This product likewise makes it is to compose your duties.

On the off chance that you are searching for cash administration programming that will permit you to make taught stock exchanges and to track your speculations, then you ought to investigate ManusRisco programming. This product is anything but difficult to utilize and permits you to settle on educated and savvy venture choices in view of your exchanging style. The product dissects different exchange conceivable outcomes and plays a positive/negative desire diversion with a specific end goal to issue you the best conceivable exchanging choice. Taking after the examination stage ManusRisco will give a full answer to help you augment your benefits. This product is intended for organizations.

The one thing that these cash administration-programming projects have in like manner is that they are all accessible on the web. You no more need to stress over moving down your PC each time you overhaul your monetary programming. These cash administration apparatuses will permit you to settle on shrewd choices with respect to your accounts and bail you escape from obligation.

How to Create a Money Management Plan

Dealing with your money gets to be much simpler in the event that you have a product system to record and break down the majority of your budgetary information. These money management programming projects can do anything from download day by day exchanges from your financial records and other venture records, help you plan and recovery toward long haul and transient objectives, and also moving in the direction of wiping out debt. Here are a few suggestions for money management programming and what they can accomplish for you.

The primary money management device that is offered online for a little month-to-month charge is the administration called Mvelopes. This product is particularly outlined as an individual home planning instrument. Mvelopes lives up to expectations comparatively to the obsolete planning device of putting trade in for cold hard currency distinctive envelopes to be utilized for diverse costs. The main contrasts are that Mvelopes offers virtual envelopes. Like Quicken, Mvelopes downloads exchanges from the greater part of your budgetary records day by day and permits you to order every exchange into particular spending classes.

At the point when contrasting Mvelopes and Quicken or Microsoft money it is anything but difficult to see the contrasts between the two. Not at all like Quicken, Mvelopes permits you to get to your own financial plan from any PC with Internet access. It additionally tracks all your credit card buys and puts aside money from each of your envelopes to pay it off every month. This highlight permits you to lessen your debt in a matter of months. With Mvelopes you can likewise pay up to 15 bills every month online for nothing. They likewise give individual planning guiding to keep you on track to achieve your objectives. The month-to-month cost for Mvelopes is $7.90. They offer a 30 free trial offer.

Another online money management programming is Gnu Cash. This administration is free and uses proficient bookkeeping standards to arrange your finances. Like other money management programming projects, Gnu Cash downloads the greater part of your money related data from the majority of your financial balances and venture accounts. It then offers an examination of your spending and sparing propensities complete with diagrams and pie outlines. This money management programming is easy to utilize and comprehend; it's much like utilizing your checkbook register. Another advantage of Cash is that you can track both individual and business finances so you don't need to have separate projects for every element. This product additionally makes it is to sort out your duties.

On the off chance that you are searching for money management programming that will permit you to make instructed stock exchanges and to track your ventures, then you ought to investigate ManusRisco programming. This product is anything but difficult to utilize and permits you to settle on educated and savvy venture choices in view of your exchanging style. The product investigates different exchange conceivable outcomes and plays a positive/negative desire diversion with a specific end goal to issue you the best conceivable exchanging choice. Taking after the examination stage ManusRisco will give a full answer to help you amplify your benefits. This product is intended for organizations.

The one thing that these money management-programming projects have in like manner is that they are all accessible on the web. You no more need to stress over moving down your PC each time you redesign your budgetary programming. These money management apparatuses will permit you to settle on savvy choices with respect to your finances and bail you escape from debt.

Money Management Means a Budget

Money Management

The vast majority accept that if they had more money the greater part of their issues would be understood. At that point they get a raise or change to a superior paying employment and their money circumstance doesn't change. They just can't comprehend why. They live in a ceaseless circle of "insufficient".

The truth of the matter is that a great many people have that EXTRA MONEY spent before they get it. How often have you heard somebody say what they are going to do with their expense discount? The same thing strives for a salary increase. Regularly, they never even notice any change in their way of life after they get the raise. The way to success is Money Management. This places you in Control.

What a great many people don't understand is that they experience the ill effects of a state of 'terminal disarray'.

This is described by a consistent condition of anxiety and feeling weak and overpowered.

Money Management

Really the response to this quandary is truly straightforward and clear. Make a BUDGET.

It is all around perceived that just around 35% of individuals have money related plans. This is on the grounds that numerous individuals are perplexed about plans.

It limits them when they discover something they need to purchase. If they realized that a financial plan is the main means for them to get what they need and make certain they can manage the cost of it. Quite a few people experience the ill effects of the motivation to purchase and this drive is fuelled by the fantasy that they can purchase when and what they need and there will be no unfavorable outcomes.

This is referred to in treatment hovers as 'Santa Clause Claus' reasoning.

Santa Clause Claus is for little kids, and this sort of intuition is not useful in being monetarily capable. Nor would it be able to prompt budgetary flourishing.

With a precisely created plan, which is money management in straightforward terms, you have money for your bills, as well as you can anticipate the things you need.

There is a great deal of WAYS TO FIND MONEY. By figuring out how to cut your current spending, you will presumably find that somewhere around 10% and 25% of your spending is superfluous. There are additionally a few money sparing sites that will issue you actually many money sparing thoughts.

More often than not it's the surprising costs that find individuals napping and make destruction with their finances. Once more, with a financial plan, you can get ready for this as well.

So in the event that you think more money will take care of your issues, simply search for it in that spot in your pay check.

Begin by keeping your numbers. This is a painstakingly composed record of all that you spend every day. It might be troublesome for you to trust that this will prompt money related thriving, however at the heart of a way of life of debating falsehoods indiscipline.

Absence of order begins in the brain and it is just here that it can be tended to. An entire lifetime of monetary flippancy can't be set backward overnight. The initial phase in the process is to keep a strict record of all your spending.

Gerry Savage is the writer of a digital book investigating and clarifying why a few individuals discover achievement while others never do. He declares that the distinction exists in the individual and his digital book and different articles show why this is so and what the individual can do about it. Getting to your potential is an educated conduct and mentality and his digital book indicates in a basic manner how this can be accomplished. We are taught to accept that change to a person is hard, however Gerry uncovers in his works how this is incorrect. He has connected these standards in his private life and helped other people to apply them, realizing monstrous change, in an extremely straightforward manner.

PPC Money Management and Blackjack

Money Management

The vast majority accept that if they had more money the greater part of their issues would be illuminated. At that point they get a raise or change to a superior paying occupation and their money circumstance doesn't change. They just can't comprehend why. They live in a never-ending circle of "insufficient".

The truth of the matter is that a great many people have that **EXTRA MONEY** spent before they get it. How frequently have you heard somebody say what they are going to do with their assessment discount? The same thing strives for a salary increase. Ordinarily, they never even notice any change in their way of life after they get the raise. The way to flourishing is Money Management. This places you in Control.

What the vast majority don't understand is that they experience the ill effects of a state of 'terminal disarray'.

This is portrayed by a steady condition of anxiety and feeling weak and overpowered.

Really the response to this issue is truly basic and clear. Make a BUDGET.

It is all around perceived that just around 35% of individuals have budgetary plans. This is on account of numerous individuals are perplexed about plans.

It limits them when they discover something they need to purchase. If they realized that a financial plan is the main means for them to get what they need and make sure they can bear the cost of it. Many individuals experience the ill effects of the drive to purchase and this motivation is fuelled by the fantasy that they can purchase when and what they need and there will be no antagonistic outcomes.

This is referred to in treatment hovers as 'Santa Clause Claus' reasoning.

Santa Clause Claus is for little kids, and this sort of intuition is not useful in being fiscally mindful. Nor would it be able to prompt money related success.

With a precisely created plan, which is money management in straightforward terms, you have money for your bills, as well as you can anticipate the things you need.

There are great deals of WAYS TO FIND MONEY. By figuring out how to cut your current spending, you will likely find that somewhere around 10% and 25% of your spending is superfluous. There are likewise a few money sparing sites that will issue you truly several money sparing thoughts.

More often than not it's the sudden costs that find individuals napping and make destruction with their finances. Once more, with a financial plan, you can anticipate this as well.

So on the off chance that you think more money will take care of your issues, simply search for it in that spot in your pay check.

Begin by keeping your numbers. This is a deliberately composed record of all that you spend once a day. It might be troublesome for you to trust that this will prompt budgetary thriving, however at the heart of a way of life of debating falsehoods indiscipline.

Absence of control begins in the brain and it is just here that it can be tended to. An entire lifetime of money related flightiness can't be set backward overnight. The initial phase in the process is to keep a strict record of all your spending.

Gerry Savage is the writer of a digital book investigating and clarifying why a few individuals discover achievement while others never do. He attests that the distinction exists in the individual and his digital book and different articles show why this is so and what the individual can do about it. Getting to your potential is a scholarly conduct and mentality and his digital book indicates in a basic manner how this can be accomplished. We are taught to accept that change to an individual is hard, however Gerry uncovers in his works how this is incorrect. He has connected these standards in his private life and helped other people to apply them, achieving enormous change, in an exceptionally straightforward manner.

Personal Money Management Guide

Personal money management guide is a secret for achieving peak productivity and maximum success in your financial life. Your attitudes influence your behaviors, which will determine what you get out of life. Setting up personal money management guide to become something greater than you currently are, is a smart way to shape your destiny. In this article I will give you a practical step by step guide on how to set up personal money management guide today.

1. Brainstorm.

Ask yourself this question — what would I do if I couldn't fail? This will get you in the proper mind state to really hone in on a compelling goal.

2. Write down your answers.

Don't censor your thoughts. Remember, you're just creating a list of things you'd like to achieve if you knew there was nothing holding you back. Write for at least 5 minutes straight. If you get stuck, ask yourself more questions. What skills do you want to master? What character traits would you like to develop in order to a personal management guide?

3. Set a budget for each goal.

Once you've written down all the things you need to do to accomplish this task, go back and read through them again. This time contact a financial planner to guide you or you can as well be your own financial planner. Write out the things you can do to avoid excess spending, whether you think you can accomplish it or not is not important. Just make a note for how to you'd like to achieve each goal. Make your goals in terms of 1, 3, 5, 10 or 20 years.

4 Get leverage- Take a few minutes to write down why you are dedicated to making this goal a reality. It will help you to start working on the goal right away, and make you more committed to achieving the goal.

If you did it right, you'll start taking action on your guide right away!

Take a few minutes to write down why you are dedicated to making this goal a reality. It will help you to start working on the goal right away, and make you more committed to achieving the goal. If you did it right, you'll start taking action on your guide right away!

Effective Money Management Tips for a Better Life

Take after these money management tips to better handle your finances and kill bill-paying anxiety. Begin the entire methodology with a record book, staying informed regarding the sum and amount of your costs. I suggest a compass of a month. Once you've assembled one-month worth of costs, sort out them into three sections. The first will be for your vital things, the second for things you don't generally require and can take out and the third for things that could give reserve funds opportunities by exchanging brands or organizations.

This ought to incorporate all bills, investment funds arrangements, **INVESTMENTS** and assessments. Having accumulated all that ought to issue you a thought of the absolute minimum that you can live on. It will be the premise for a lean month-to-month plan. Making it excessively strict will overcome the reason, as you won't stick to it. You need to remove however much waste as could reasonably be expected yet issue yourself a little elbowroom. Issuing yourself a little month-to-month recompense to spend too much on anything you covet can finish this.

Contingent upon your circumstances and pay you may begin with 25 or 50 dollars a month. From that point on, get into the propensity for observing your genuine spending against your financial plan and make adjustments when required. On the off chance that you consider every one of its advantages, planning is one of the money management tips excessively couple of individuals consider important.

Next, check out you and see what you can save money on. For example:

Utilize an auto spread if your auto isn't stopped in a carport. You will ensure it, not require auto washes as regularly and won't spend as much on support. Presently for money management tips with respect to your superfluous ways of managing money: Do you have to go out twice a week?. Figure out how to cook and you will spare a ton. Not every new motion picture ought to be unquestionable requirements see. Endure until it goes ahead DVD. Don't quit doing everything; simply discover a superior (less expensive) method for doing certain things and farthest point your pointless trips. Shorten any lavish interests, for example, snowboarding or hitting the fairway. You can begin by skirting each other outing. Not getting a snowboarding pass can spare you hundreds. You could spare considerably more on the off chance that you leave the golf clubs at home.

Money Management

Over and over again, we rampages spend on getting the most current innovations. This incorporates feature recreations, upgraded PC programming, or actually getting another cell like clockwork. Leasing the amusement or holding up six months till the new tech toy descends in cost in not the apocalypse. With the snappy propel in innovation its practically ruinous to stay aware of everything, so why not hold up and skirt each other overhaul? Pay down debt with the money you'll spare. One of the best things you can do to spare money is to quit smoking and drinking. It's undesirable and can prompt immense future doctors visit expenses. One more of the money management tips regularly disregarded is to quit betting. Regardless of the fact that you just burn through 5 dollars a week on A LOTTO ticket, it adds up to 20 dollars a month or 240 dollars a year. Add to that any wagering with companions or on donning occasions and the expense could be significant. Indeed, even a week after week bingo propensity can include. Pay every one of your bills on time. Expecting you are fined 30 dollars with a late expense on a bill, if this happens with three charges a couple of times each year, you'll be discarding a little fortune. Continuously be on time, pay on line, and put electronic alarms for your bills. Your credit and the general strength of your finances will move forward.

Escape from debt as quick as possible. Again and again, individuals pile on credit card unpaid liability on things as straightforward as a plane ticket for an excursion and after that doesn't pay it off. It's so helpful it would be impossible pay the base. Comprehend that credit card organizations alter your base so that just piece of your installment goes to the sum owed and the other part goes to hobby. You can wind up paying twice or three times the measure of all that you put on credit. By taking after these straightforward money management tips you can spare a considerable measure and significantly enhance you're finances.

When Money Management Habits Need A Boost

Albeit nobody embarks to wind up in noteworthy debt, it does happen. Whether your debt issues are the consequence of your poor money management abilities or an unforeseen life circumstance, there is still bounty to find out about individual debt. One of the greatest territories in need of change for a great many people is figuring out how to perceive when finances turn into an issue. After that it just requires a little training and push to build up an arrangement that attempts to determine debt inconveniences and have a fiscally solid future.

Pitiful Savers

Exploration demonstrates that the dominant part of Americans have almost no reserve funds. Indeed, fewer than 33% of families have enough money spared to pay their bills in the occasion of work misfortune or hiccup in wage. With so couple of individuals arranged for a stormy day, it is no big surprise that debt weights sneak up effortlessly. A decent general guideline is to have no less than four to six months worth of costs spared to take care of the expenses of vital livings costs, for example, a home loan, auto, gas and perishables, anything not as much as this can rapidly transform an impermanent money related hardship into a staggering debt issue. Sparing ought to be a need, not a bit of hindsight. At the point when sparing money isn't a piece of an organized plan, it may flag a more serious issue.

Awful Budgeting

Are we awful at sparing, as well as the majority of us don't have a financial plan. This implies that numerous individuals are working every month without a definite thought of where their money is going and the amount they have left for the rest of the month. Sketching out and taking after a financial plan is a standout amongst the most important money related instruments we can possess. While it does require some serious energy and exertion, keeping a nearby eye on the monetary allowance is the most ideal approach to counteract overspending. Further, planning takes into consideration us to perceive designs in our spending and recognize ranges in which we can roll out improvements. There are numerous online and PDA devices accessible to help make planning simple.

Senseless Spending

Let's be honest, we all purchase things we don't require now and again. This propensity is not inalienably dangerous until it meddles with planning and sparing. Most Americans perceive credit cards as a device of accommodation, not budgetary arranging. Credit cards shouldn't be utilized to buy things rapidly or that one can't bear, yet rather to support credit and monetary standing. This implies that to utilize a credit card carefully we must arrangement our buys, know the amount we can bear the cost of and just utilize the credit card with the end goal of building ourselves as capable borrowers. Having more than three credit cards, or cards conveying offsets higher than 40 percent of as far as possible, flags an issue. The objective here is to decrease credit card debt and start to utilize the cards irregularly for things that we can bear to pay off in a couple of months time.

Tips on Money Management During Economic Recession

Albeit nobody embarks to wind up in huge debt, it does happen. Whether your debt issues are the aftereffect of your poor money management aptitudes or an unforeseen life circumstance, there is still bounty to find out about individual debt. The subsidence requires a strict watch on your own finances and plan. Amid these extreme times you have to be shrewd in money management so as to secure your finances. This is a period when you may confront a lessening in salary. On the other hand, with a couple of safety measures you can wind up beating the subsidence and keep up a sound money related status.

A standout amongst the most imperative errands in money management is to check your ledger routinely and stay informed concerning each announcement. The key is to set aside a few minutes so you don't wind up paying hobby. This is likewise the time to quit fooling around about your financial plan and lessen day by day costs as much as you can. Amid a retreat you won't need your own reserve funds to get destroyed. Along these lines, keep a record of each penny spent and begin sparing. This is not the time

Money Management

to get into credit card debt either. Convey your credit card in the event that you should, yet doesn't wind up swiping it on pointless things that you can without much of a stretch manage without. Even better, keep you credit cards away. It would be judicious to keep the least intrigue card entirely for crises. Since they convey the most elevated interest rates you could wind up in genuine debt on the off chance that you start to default on installments.

One of the most intelligent things in money management amid a subsidence is not to obtain money. Regardless of the possibility that a bank offers the most alluring premium rates, you can just sink more profound into debt and never have the capacity to happen to retreat with a sound budgetary standing when you have credits to clear amid these intense times. Be that as it may, verify you pay your protection premiums on time. They are the best security and inability to make general installments may put at hazard the sum you have effectively paid. Subsequently, it bodes well to pay your premiums and take out any protection dangers.

A subsidence is a period when you should search for distinctive wellsprings of salary if conceivable. On the off chance that you can deal with tackling additional occupations, regardless of how little they are, you can expand your own wage and have the capacity to plan your month to month costs effortlessly. Extreme circumstances call for difficult measures and your additional endeavors will most likely pay rich profits. At the point when looking for goods and different essentials it pays to shop with rebate coupons and voucher codes. You will discover a lot of them on the web. Indeed, even a 10 percent discount can go far in helping you spare money.

The way to effective money management amid retreat is to diminish your spending and debt too. On the off chance that you can figure out how to deal with these two perspectives, your own finances will get an incredible help. In particular, you will have the capacity to stay one stage in front of the retreat. When you make a sensible plan verify you stick to it. Preferably you have to have the capacity to spare around 40 percent of your pay. In the event that you haven't possessed the capacity to accomplish that, make it your first fleeting money related objective.

Dismal Savers

Examination demonstrates that the dominant part of Americans have next to no funds. Truth be told, under 33% of families have enough money spared to pay their bills in the occasion of work misfortune or hiccup in salary. With so couple of individuals arranged for a stormy day, it is no big surprise that debt weights sneak up effortlessly. A decent dependable guideline is to have no less than four to six months worth of costs spared to take care of the expenses of key livings costs, for example, a home loan, auto, gas and perishables, anything not as much as this can rapidly transform a brief money related hardship into an overwhelming debt issue. Sparing ought to be a need, not an idea in retrospect. At the point when sparing money isn't a piece of an organized plan, it may flag a more concerning issue.

Terrible Budgeting

Are we terrible at sparing, as well as the greater part of us doesn't have a financial plan. This implies that numerous individuals are working every month without any thought of where their money is going and the amount they have left for the rest of the month. Plotting and taking after a financial plan is a standout amongst the most important monetary apparatuses we can possess. While it does require significant investment and exertion, keeping a nearby eye on the monetary allowance is the most ideal approach to avert overspending. Further, planning takes into consideration us to perceive designs in our spending and recognize territories in which we can roll out improvements. There are numerous online and advanced cell apparatuses accessible to help make planning simple.

Senseless Spending

Let's be honest, we all purchase things we don't require every now and then. This propensity is not inalienably hazardous until it meddles with planning and sparing. Most Americans perceive credit cards as a device of accommodation, not monetary arranging. Credit cards shouldn't be utilized to buy things rapidly or that one can't manage, but instead to help credit and budgetary standing. This implies that to utilize a credit card carefully we must arrangement our buys, know the amount we can manage the cost of and just utilize the credit card with the end goal of creating ourselves as mindful borrowers. Having more than three credit cards, or cards conveying equalizations higher than 40 percent of as far as possible, flags an issue. The objective here is to diminish credit card debt and start to utilize the cards irregularly for things that we can bear to pay off in a couple of months time.

Money Management Tips For Career Changers

There frequently comes a period in life when you get to be bolstered up of the schedule that you have made for yourself. Adjusting work and family can be a battle and that is the reason numerous individuals don't generally consider changing their employments; regardless of the amount they may detest it. Nonetheless, some of the time in life, you need to go for broke keeping in mind the end goal to be cheerful and changing professions may be precisely what you have to kick begin your life once more.

Can Money Management Help You?

One of the principle reasons why individuals don't take after their fantasies is an absence of money. Such a variety of individuals are stuck working in a dull employment in light of the fact that they feel that they can't stand to surrender it and would what they like to do. Truly changing professions can influence your finances, yet there are routes in which you can get around it. By adapting all the more about money management, you can help to show signs of improvement position monetarily so as to change your profession.

It is about being arranged and in the event that you need something seriously enough, you have to get ready for it. So in the event that you need another profession and you are not certain that you can bear to roll out the improvement–then set aside!

Approaches To Manage Your Money

A few routes in which you can guarantee that you can be monetarily secure when you roll out the improvement include:

Curtailing Luxuries

Endeavoring to Save

Taking a College Course to Gain New Skills

The above are simply a couple of routes in which you can deal with your money. By taking a school course, for instance, you can learn new aptitudes which will successfully guarantee that when you are prepared to move onto another employment, you will get paid more for it.

The primary route in which you can spare, then again, is by curtailing different things every month. By working out what you are spending and where you are spending it, you can see precisely where you may have the capacity to spare money.

Case in point, might you be able to spare money on nourishment? Do you permit yourself day by day treats which you could possibly reduce? Do you eat out a great deal? On the off chance that so you may have the capacity to chop down and spare a minimal expenditure simultaneously. It is stunning the amount of money you could spare by simply curtailing a bit.

You additionally must be prepared to put resources into your fantasy vocation. This implies that you have to spare as much money as you agreeably can. Open up a bank account and begin sparing immediately. Put in as much as you can bear the cost of every month and you will soon begin to see it mounting up.

With a specific end goal to effectively have the capacity to bear to change professions, you do need to partake in great money management. By setting aside, you can undoubtedly make the move to your fantasy work with almost no issue.

Tips on Personal Finance and Debt Management

On the off chance that you are in debt, you have to diminish and in the end pass your debt first before whatever else. The way to debt diminishment and disposal is your own dedication and control. The ventures for debt lessening and disposal are exceptionally straightforward. The test is to continue through to the end.

Stop Further Debt

Extreme acquiring is the reason for most debt issues. You ought to just obtain what you truly require. Keeping fitting records of your debt and don't dismiss your goals. Your debt ought to be for the transient and you ought to intend to clear them inside a couple of months. Don't let your advances inflatable into debt issue.

Diminish Your Expenditures

Make this a fixation. In the event that you take the transport or train to work as opposed to driving, salute yourself on the money you are saving money on gas and stopping. On the off chance that you have stuffed lunch as opposed to burning through money at the cafeteria or lavish eatery, salute yourself. You would have set aside to $3000 a year. Money that will go to diminishing your debt.

Lessen Your Debt

Attempt to merge your debts and secure a lower interest rate. Begin paying more than the base whole and set a deadline to pass your debt. This is the best way to decrease your debts. To attain to this, you require a legitimate plan.

Make a Monthly Budget

A standout amongst the best and essential money management devices is the financial backing. Concocting a financial plan is genuinely basic however you have to have the control to stick to it. A financial plan is basically a timetable of your procuring and what you have to spend. The essential words here are "what you have to spend". Be judicious and thrifty with your money, you are now in debt, what other reason do you require? The way to great individual finance management is to spend inside your methods. To check drive spending, have a go at leaving your credit cards at home.

Get Into a Debt Settlement Program

In the event that you incurred a tremendous debt, consider getting into a debt settlement program. On the off chance that you need to do it without anyone's help, you simply need to contact your creditors to advise them about your arrangement for debt settlement. Most budgetary establishments are interested in debt settlement proposition so you ought not delay to approach them for better terms. Most money related organizations will permits up to 40% to 60% diminishment on credits sum payable. Arrangements can be very dubious so you can think about procuring as a debt settlement organization in the event that you are not up to it.

Debt Reduction-Money Management

Maybe one of your New Year's objectives is to get on track with your finances, and start to build up a significantly more fiscally sound way of life. This is really an extremely regular New Year's Resolution, however not one that everybody stays with. The purposes behind this are abundant yet it comes down to several things. Debt is anything but difficult to wrack up, hard to dispose of- and when you have existing costs that must be paid; now and again it is anything but difficult to get behind. Not simply here and there, more often than not, really. Individuals observe that they build up debt and afterward, just can't get pull out, yet, with a touch of planning, arranging and the right disposition, it can be somewhat to a lesser degree a battle.

For one thing, you're going to need to face the entirety of all that you have to pay off. Both regarding debt, and as far as month-to-month costs. This is the hardest piece of the whole money management arrangement on the grounds that it can be totally disheartening. Nonetheless, whoever you are, wherever you will be, you can wager there is somebody who might be listening, presumably numerous individuals out there who has had much more regrettable debt than you do, and have figured out how to escape from that. So remember as you take a gander at your rundown this is simply everything. What you're truly going to do is break this tremendous pile of an objective down into littler objectives that will be a great deal all the more simple to concentrate on, as well as achieve so that you likewise construct your trust in having the capacity to tackle the whole thing, a tad at once.

The second thing, get control of your in the now going through with a financial plan. When you do have that in rigging, you have a much clearer picture of what you can do about the debt issue. On the off chance that you've got a financial plan, it ordinarily starts with following where your money goes- the zones that you can reduce, do. Pare it down to essentials and the incidental break. It's critical that you not totally reduced out recreational fun- however you may need to discover less expensive approaches to get that unwinding in, on the off chance that you can. Since you've done that, now is the ideal time to make a few calls.

Beginning with the debts that have a 15 percent interest rate or more- call them and arrange a bring down one. This is the thing that a credit management firm would do- but on the other hand it's something that you can do. On the off chance that you can't get them to lower and you can deal with an exchange offer? Do as such. If not, you should seriously mull over making this your first objective, in the event that you feel you can handle that one immediately. Somehow, you'll deal with this debt. These are the first ventures to taking back control over your money. It might be a long voyage, yet it is most likely one that is justified regardless of your time and vitality and more than that, its one that is surely feasible for you.

Money Management for Wealth Building

Riches building isn't muddled yet how we management our money is by all accounts. The essential rule is to spend short of what we make and set aside some of that money for what's to come. Not muddled, isn't that so?

Notwithstanding, we appear to have gotten ourselves into a somewhat of a pickle in the course of the most recent decade or something like that. I think we never thought there would be any issue with paying off our debt. Indeed, things didn't go as we arranged and now we need to manage getting ourselves out of a monstrous debt load. Possibly my guardians had it right: set aside 10% of all that you make, let it win premium and when you resign you will have enough money to bolster yourself for whatever remains of your life. It worked for my guardians yet tragically I thought they had an exhausting life and I needed things.

Today I have figured out how to do things another way with my money. I've set a financial plan for myself and discovered that financial plans aren't exhausting and that I have more money toward the end of the month than I use to have.

Here are a couple of dependable tips on the best way to manufacture riches:

Set a financial plan and stick to it. It may not be glitzy yet it meets expectations. Take your salary for the month, subtract regardless of your costs including putting no less than 10% for investment funds.

Diminish your costs. Do you truly require another pair of shoes? On the off chance that you can stand to purchase them yet needn't bother with them, put the money in an investment account. Each time you consider purchasing something you truly needn't bother with, put the money away. You'll be amazed the amount of money you have in your investment account toward the end of the year.

Offer things you're not utilizing. This is an extraordinary approach to get SOME EXTRA CASH. Have a yard deal or offer the things on Craigslist.

Dispose of debt. There are two or three approaches to dispose of debt. On the off chance that you have a ton and you would prefer not to opt for non-payment see a debt solidification organization to help you. They can arrange with your creditors to have the interest lessened or extend the time you need to pay off the debt. On the off chance that you need to deal with paying off your debt yourself then attempt the "snowball technique". You begin by paying off the littlest bill first while keeping on paying the base on the various bills. When that bill is paid take the money you have been paying to it and apply it to the following littlest sum. Proceed with this methodology until every one of your bills is current.

Request a settlement. On the off chance that you don't inquire as to whether this could work. Contact your creditors and attempt to arrange a settlement with them. This system can be fruitful with more seasoned debt, for example, understudy advances.

Eight Money Management Essentials

Effective money management doesn't have to be confused. Then again, in spite of the fact that the steps may be basic, it obliges a ton of restraint and determination. How about we examine the 10 essential standards on how you can take better control of your FINANCES and keep away from debt issues.

1. be mindful of your monetary circumstance. Having a sensible perspective of your monetary circumstance can help you settle on better money related choices. To get an exact assessment, figure all your month to month costs starting from the largest to the littlest penny. Include every one of your uses and look at the outcome from your MONTHLY INCOME. Is there money left to pay off your debts? Is there enough money left to put in your reserve funds?

2. be mindful of your debts. Precisely what amount of debt do you owe your creditors? Acquire a duplicate of your credit report and precisely check your charges. In the event that there are wrong charges in your report, you can debate them with your creditor or with the credit authorities. In the event that

all charges in your records are right, focus the precise measure of debt have and make a reimbursement arrangement.

3. Save your money. This may appear glaringly evident yet shockingly, numerous individuals have a tendency to ignore or disregard this vital step. Every month, make it a propensity to set aside a part of your pay for your investment account. You ought to additionally set aside your own just-in-case account that you can use for startling costs.

4. Prioritize your costs. You ought to first pay consideration on your necessities. In the event that your salary is insufficient to cover for every one of your uses, you may need to surrender the less critical or immaterial things. Case in point, you may decide to subscribe to a lower arrangement of web, link or PDA. Keep in mind, making little yields spares you from the agony and inconvenience that awful debt can bring.

5. Exercise control with your credit card utilization. In the event that you have CREDIT CARDS, use them with alert. Make it a point to pay off your offset totally before charging new buys. Utilize your card just for essential buys. In the event that you must utilize your card, keep away from the extra intrigue rate and late punishment charges by paying off your whole adjust before your due date.

6. Pay every one of your bills on time. Late installments can altogether indicate your costs. You can stay away from all these additional expenses by basically presenting your installments on time. On the off chance that you can't make it on your due date, summon your creditor right and educate them of your circumstance. Request an expansion. Most creditors would give thought on the off chance that you advise them ahead of time.

7. Set long haul objectives. Shouldn't we think about your long terms objectives? Money related specialist's guidance securing individual and therapeutic protection scope for you and your crew. Add to your retirement arrange particularly if your head honcho offers a 401kfund.

8. Create a reasonable plan. Planning your MONTHLY INCOME is vital. Separate your wage between your debts, service bills, individual costs and reserve funds. A financial plan arrangement would help you consider which costs you can slice off from your rundown.

Budget and Credit Counseling

On the off chance that you are encountering monetary issues, and battling with debt, then plan and credit directing could be the start of the way out. There are offices that spend significant time in taking a gander at individual budgetary circumstances, and serving to plan a financial plan to discover methods for passing your debt. These administrations right now help various distinctive individuals in this kind of circumstance every single day.

To advantage from credit directing you initially need to do your examination into an administration that would be suitable for you. This implies taking sooner or later to research whether the advising administration charges for their assistance. There are numerous non-benefit associations accessible however you ought to consider the way that there may at present be shrouded charges which you ought to verify you are mindful of.

When you go to directing arrangements its imperative frankly about the majority of your money related inconveniences. Giving the organization however much data as could reasonably be expected will imply that you have the absolute best risk of discovering a way out of your inconveniences and have the capacity to pay off your debts snappier. When you give this data, you will be taught approaches to deal with your debt and arrangement your financial plan effectively. Quality debt advisors will really help you build up a debt management plan and plan.

Financial plan and credit guiding is an incredible method for escaping from debt, and additionally realizing all the money management aptitudes you have to guarantee you don't incur some significant debt once more. Verify you discover a trustworthy guiding administration who is truly intrigued by helping you, and you will be well while in transit to getting to be debt free.

Options for Money Management Help

In terms of money, everybody encounters their own money taking care of issues, whether rich or poor. Trust it or not, even the individuals who have rich money think that it hard to deal with their finances.

Money is a genuine matter on the grounds that regardless, you NEED MONEY so as to survive; notwithstanding, the miserable truth is that not all can deal with money legitimately. There are a few individuals who might frequently burn through money until they go bankrupt and ask money from companions and relatives. As opposed to getting used to this wrong demeanor, it would be best to endeavor and figure out how to deal with your finances properly.

To help you in dealing with your money, you ought to consider the administrations of a money related master. Begin searching for a monetary advisor inside your group and you will doubtlessly have the capacity to discover somebody. Normally, you can discover budgetary guiding help through your bank however it can likewise be accessible through courses or by looking for a monetary master. Be that as it may, on the off chance that you need help through individual examination, then you ought to realize that it accompanies a charge. This is the reason it is imperative to assemble a rundown of potential money counselors and check who among the rundown is dependable and would fit your financial plan.

On the off chance that you don't have enough money to pay for an individual mentor, you can benefit free money management strategies through courses. Continuously check your group notice and check whether there are timetables for courses that examine this matter. Nonetheless, these workshops would just show you the rudiments and you may discover them hard to apply in your own finances particularly in the event that you don't comprehend the ideas that much.

Concerning the individuals who have EXTRA MONEY, they look for the administrations of a specialist money management mentor on the grounds that this is more valuable over the long haul.

With a dependable finance master, you can be guaranteed with your money. The master can give you guidance on choice profiting. Contracting a specialist to issue you an exhortation about taking care of your money matters can be a decent venture on the grounds that when you have the capacity to handle your finances legitimately, you will most likely get benefits later on.

While a few individuals may imagine that money taking care of is not that troublesome, it is still fitting to look for master exhortation. A legitimately oversaw FINANCE can bring about less push and less stresses; in this way, helping you to unwind and appreciate life.

Money Management With No Excuses

Your business is there to sustain you, and food you well, in the event that you need. However there is a great deal you have to think about your business with a specific end goal to get the financials right.

Begin by making sense of what you require monetarily. At that point, go to your business and say, "Business, this is the thing that I require." You must be willing to do the work needed to have your business convey this to you.

Robert Kiyosaki, best known as the creator of Rich Dad, Poor Dad, says, "Neglecting to plan is wanting to fall flat." When he discusses coming up short, he's not so much looking at going bankrupt. Another meaning of disappointment is keeping you down or staying static, and this is regularly the consequence of an absence of arranging.

Arranging includes comprehending what frameworks and components you have to have set up, for example,

The numbers- From a monetary angle, you must comprehend a couple of basic numbers-your essential overhead (what it expenses to maintain your business, including your hourly rate), your benefit (what you procure well beyond your costs) and your financial plans (spending projections in view of income projections)-before you can begin estimating an undertaking.

Bookkeeping, charging and gathering- It's fundamental to have a framework set up so you can keep close track of where your time and money goes. (There is programming to do that; we suggest Function Fox.) Everything that comes in and goes out ought to be archived. You may require an accountant to come in routinely to do accounting or charging, or possibly to administer what you are doing and verify you're doing it right.

Business arrangements, installment terms and conditions- You are in the driver's seat here. Don't sit tight for your customers to let you know how to maintain your business. One of the advantages of being independently employed is that you get the chance to decide how (and regularly the amount) you need to be paid. You get the chance to choose what to do when amazements happen, for example, the retraction of an occupation or a quarter century of corrections. This must all be spelled out ahead of time and included in your agreement.

The research material- Memories are woefully insufficient; so don't even attempt to depend on yours in terms of the assertions you make with your customers. Rather, set up a basic documentation framework with layouts for recommendations, contracts, appraisals, letters of assentation, calendars, courses of events and change arranges that your customers will approve. This sets an expert tone right from the earliest starting point of any business relationship. On the off chance that you neglect to foundation this procedure at the beginning, it's significantly more difficult to place frameworks set up later on.

With a specific end goal to set objectives and focus a financial plan, you must work out what you have to gain, as well as how that number interprets into the quantity of customers you require, and how that deciphers into the amount of promoting you must do to accomplish that.

As such, what number of proposition do you need to present every month keeping in mind the end goal to make your numbers? What number of calls (frosty or warm) should you make to be requested that number of proposition? What number of prospects do you require in your pipeline to get that number of appeals for proposition?

Without taking the time to work this out for yourself, its far-fetched you'll attain to your objectives.

Besides, without this data, you won't know when to venture up your advertising, when to go to one additionally organizing occasion, when to make a round of subsequent gets or when to convey an additional pamphlet.

Money Management

In our day and time, it is constantly great to know how to spare your money, and profit. To assist you, we have assembled a rundown of proposals to help you do simply that. It obliges a little time, and exertion, yet the advantages will be well justified, despite all the trouble. So keep perusing to figure out how you can better your current budgetary circumstance.

Money Management: Learn To Save Your Money

A critical venture in dealing with your money is to first take in the significance of sparing money. This could be possible by figuring out how to plan your regular income. After some time you will start to perceive the amount you spend, and it will help you to spare more money. A financial plan is discriminating for appropriately dealing with your finances, so make it a top need for your family unit.

Next, you may need to start utilizing an online bank account. By utilizing this sort of record, you will be less inclined to utilize it once a day. When you have an investment funds, it will issue you more trust later on. Case in point, ought to a crisis circumstance emerge, you can simply fall back on your funds, rather than your credit cards.

Money Management: HOW TO MAKE MONEY

You can likewise take in the focal point of HOW TO MAKE MONEY on the web. This could be possible any number of ways. The colossal thing about profiting on the web is the straightforward actuality that you can profit from the solace of your home. The critical thing is to discover an outlet that you really appreciate. So take as much time as required, and audit your alternatives.

A couple of cases of how you can MAKE MONEY ONLINE are figuring out how to assemble sites, and web illustrations. You can likewise get paid you blog for organizations, and different assets. Another extraordinary choice is to round out paid overviews with respect to items that you have utilized as a part of the past. These are every single astounding asset for you to gain an additional pay.

Money Management: Final Thoughts

Figure out how to make these strides each one in turn, and before you know it you will procure the numerous prizes of an all around oversaw money related future. On the off chance that you have discovered that MAKING MONEY is optional to escaping from debt, or perhaps you are only up the creek without a paddle, then you may need to consider a non-benefit credit advising administration. They will work with you to help you get back on track.

WAIT! – DO YOU LIKE FREE BOOKS?

My FREE Gift to You!! As a way to say Thank You for downloading my book, I'd like to offer you more FREE BOOKS! Each time we release a NEW book, we offer it first to a small number of people as a test - drive. Because of your commitment here in downloading my book, I'd love for you to be a part of this group. You can join easily here ➔ http://yourcashmanagement.com/

Conclusion

Thank you again for downloading this book!

If you enjoyed this book, then I'd like to ask you for a favor, would you be kind enough to leave a review for this book on Amazon? It'd be greatly appreciated!

Help us better serve you by sending questions or comments to greatreadspublishing@gmail.com - Thank you!